Ashley

READING/WRITING
COMPANION

Mc
Graw
Hill
Education

COVER: Nathan Love, Erwin Madrid

mheducation.com/prek-12

Send all inquiries to:
McGraw-Hill Education
Two Penn Plaza
New York, NY 10121

ISBN: 978-0-07-901854-0
MHID: 0-07-901854-8

Printed in the United States of America.

8 9 10 11 12 13 14 SWI 26 25 24 23 22   C

Welcome to Wonders!

Read exciting **Literature**, **Science**, and **Social Studies** texts!

★ **LEARN** about the world around you!

★ **THINK**, **SPEAK**, and **WRITE** about genres!

★ **COLLABORATE** in discussion and inquiry!

★ **EXPRESS** yourself!

my.mheducation.com
Use your student login to read core texts, practice grammar and spelling, explore research projects and more!

GENRE STUDY 1 **EXPOSITORY TEXT**

SCIENCE

GENRE STUDY 2 **REALISTIC FICTION**

GENRE STUDY **3 ARGUMENTATIVE TEXT**

WRAP UP THE UNIT

Kwaku Alston/Stockland Martel

 **Digital Tools** Find this eBook and other resources at **my.mheducation.com**

v

GENRE STUDY 1 **EXPOSITORY TEXT**

SCIENCE

GENRE STUDY 2 **DRAMA**

GENRE STUDY 3 POETRY

WRAP UP THE UNIT

 Digital Tools Find this eBook and other resources at **my.mheducation.com**

Natural disasters are events such as hurricanes, earthquakes, floods, and forest fires. These events cause a huge crisis in a community. Fortunately, there are people who are trained to respond to these challenges.

Look at the photograph. Then talk to a partner about what you might do to help after a natural disaster. In the chart, write some ways people might respond during natural disasters.

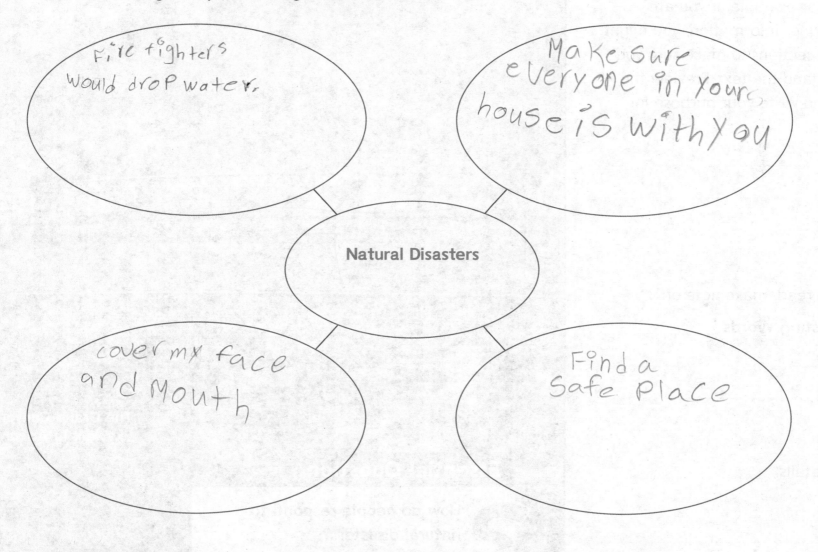

Fire fighters would drop water.

Make sure everyone in your house is with you

Natural Disasters

cover my face and Mouth

Find a Safe Place

Go online to **my.mheducation.com** and read the "Masters of Disasters" Blast. What do you think is the most important characteristic of a first responder? Blast back your response.

Masterfile

TAKE NOTES

Understanding why you are reading helps you adjust how you read. For example, if you are reading for information, you might reread sections to make sure you understand the text. Preview the text and write your purpose for reading.

_____

_____

_____

_____

As you read, make note of:

Interesting Words _____

_____

_____

_____

Key Details _____

_____

_____

_____

A World of CHANGE

The Grand Canyon Skywalk in Arizona

Essential Question

How do people respond to natural disasters?

Read about how people prepare for natural disasters.

image100/Corbis

Earth may seem as if it is a large rock that never changes. Actually, our planet is in a constant state of change. Natural changes take place every day. These activities **alter** the surface of Earth. Some of these changes take place slowly over many years. Others happen in just minutes. Whether they are slow or fast, both kinds of changes have a great effect on our planet.

Slow and Steady

Some of Earth's biggest changes can't be seen. That is because they are happening very slowly. Weathering, erosion, and deposition are three natural processes that change the surface of the world. They do it one grain of sand at a time.

Weathering occurs when rain, snow, sun, and wind break down rocks into smaller pieces. These tiny pieces of rock turn into soil, but they are not carried away from the landform.

Erosion occurs when weathered pieces of rock are carried away by a natural force such as a river. This causes landforms on Earth to get smaller. They may even completely **collapse** over time. The Grand Canyon is an example of the effect of erosion. It was carved over thousands of years by the Colorado River.

After the process of erosion, dirt and rocks are then dropped in a new location. This process is called deposition. Over time, a large collection of deposits may occur in one place. Deposition by water can build up a beach. Deposition by wind can create a **substantial** landform, such as a sand dune.

Julie Quarry / Alamy Stock Photo

FIND TEXT EVIDENCE

Read

Paragraph 1
Compare and Contrast
Underline the words that tell how some natural changes are different from other natural changes.

Paragraphs 2–5
Reread
Circle the three natural processes that slowly change Earth's surface.

Draw a box around the words that explain how the Grand Canyon was formed. What happens to dirt and rocks after the process of erosion? Write it here.

The dirt and rock moves somewhere else.

Reread

Author's Craft

How does the author show you the causes and effects of natural processes?

FIND TEXT EVIDENCE 🔍

Read

Paragraphs 1–3

Compare and Contrast

Underline the three different ways people try to stop beach erosion. Write them here.

① build structures

② use havy rocks

③ grow Plants

Paragraphs 4–5

Reread

Draw a box around the text that explains why volcanic eruptions and landslides are called natural disasters. **Circle** words that explain how magma moves.

What can happen when an eruption occurs without warning?

They can cause a crisis

Reread

Author's Craft

How does the author use headings to give and organize information?

Although erosion is a slow process, it still creates problems for people. Some types of erosion are dangerous. They can be seen as a **hazard** to communities.

To help protect against beach erosion, people build structures that block ocean waves from the shore. They may also use heavy rocks to keep the land from eroding. Others grow plants along the shore. The roots of the plants help hold the soil and make it less likely to erode.

Unfortunately, people cannot protect the land when fast natural processes occur.

Fast and Powerful

Fast natural processes, like slow processes, change the surface of Earth. But fast processes are much more powerful. They are often called natural disasters because of the **destruction** they cause. Volcanic eruptions and landslides are just two examples.

Volcanoes form around openings in Earth's crust. When pressure builds under Earth's surface, hot melted rock called magma is forced upwards. It flows up through the volcano and out through the opening. Eruptions can occur without warning. They have the potential to cause a **crisis** in a community.

Like volcanic eruptions, landslides can happen without warning. They occur when rocks and dirt, loosened by heavy rains, slide down a hill or mountain. Some landslides are small. Others can be quite large and cause **severe** damage.

Be Prepared

In contrast to slow-moving processes, people cannot prevent the effects of fast-moving natural disasters. Instead, scientists try to predict when these events will occur so that they can warn people. Still, some disasters are **unpredictable** and strike without warning. It is important for communities to have an emergency plan in place so that they can be evacuated quickly.

The surface of Earth constantly changes through natural processes. These processes can be gradual or swift. They help to make Earth the amazing planet that it is!

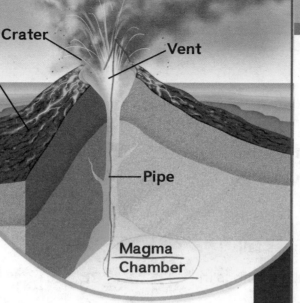

Cone   Crater   Vent

Pipe

Magma Chamber

Westend01/Getty Images

Summarize

Use your notes, the diagram, and the images to help you summarize "A World of Change." Compare slow and fast changes to Earth's surface.

FIND TEXT EVIDENCE

> Read

Paragraphs 1–3
Multiple-Meaning Words

In the second sentence in paragraph 1, the word *slide* is used as a verb. **Underline** context clues that help give the meaning. What is another meaning for *slide*?

a tool on a play ground

Diagrams

Look at the diagram. How does the magma travel through the volcano? Write it here.

It goes from a magma chamber toethe pipe and out and out the vent.

> Reread

Author's Craft

What is the author's purpose for writing the section "Be Prepared"?

Vocabulary

Use the example sentences to talk with a partner about each word. Then answer the questions.

alter
The storm will **alter** the park if many trees fall.

What kinds of storms have you seen alter things in your state?

snowostorm, rainstorm state

collapse
Floodwaters caused the bridge to **collapse**!

What might cause a tent to collapse?

Tree+win-tower collanps.
rain
wind

crisis
Rescue workers help people during an emergency or **crisis**, such as a flood.

What other event might be a crisis?

when someone breaks a leg its a crisis. Tornado Fire

destruction
The dogs ran through the store, causing a lot of damage and **destruction**.

How can wind cause destruction?

It can blow stuff down. wire fall Powersgoes down

hazard
That broken step is a **hazard** because someone might fall!

What else might be a hazard?

A hurracaip is a hazard. broken glass Lost shoe latses

 Build Your Word List Pick one of the interesting words you noted on page 2 and look up its meaning. Then work with a partner to make a word web of synonyms, antonyms, and related words. Use a thesaurus to help you find words.

severe

Severe weather can include very strong winds and heavy rain.

What kinds of severe weather has your state had?

[handwritten] hurrican earsandy it happen on 22 octuber 2012.

[handwritten] Hurrican ice blizzard

substantial

A **substantial** number of parents came to the meeting.

What is a synonym for *substantial*?

[handwritten] same

[handwritten] A substantial of People Who live in a state.

[handwritten] a lot   big amant

unpredictable

The **unpredictable** weather suddenly changed from sunny to rainy.

What is an antonym for *unpredictable*?

[handwritten] People can unpredict what is going to be the weather on a day.

[handwritten] predict Know it will happen

Multiple-Meaning Words

Some words may have more than one meaning. To figure out the meaning of a multiple-meaning word, check the words and phrases near it for clues.

FIND TEXT EVIDENCE

There are a few different meanings for the word block, *so it is a multiple-meaning word. The word* protect *and the phrase* "ocean waves from the shore" *help me figure out that the meaning for the word* block *in this sentence is* "stop."

To help protect against beach erosion, people build structures that block ocean waves from the shore.

Your Turn Use context clues to figure out the meanings of the following words in "A World of Change."

place, *page 3, paragraph 1* _____

_____

shore, *page 4, paragraph 2* _____

_____

Reread

When you read an expository text, you may come across facts and ideas that are new to you. As you read "A World of Change," you can reread the difficult sections to make sure you understand them and to help you remember key details.

🔍 FIND TEXT EVIDENCE

You may not be sure why a volcano erupts. Reread the section "Fast and Powerful" on page 4 of "A World of Change."

Page 4

Volcanoes form around openings in Earth's crust. When pressure builds under Earth's surface, hot melted rock called magma is forced upwards. It flows up through the volcano and out through the opening. Eruptions can occur without warning. They have the potential to cause a **crisis** in a community.

I read that when pressure builds under Earth's surface, magma is forced upwards. From this I can draw the inference that pressure below the surface causes a volcano to erupt.

Your Turn What happens to rock during weathering? Reread the section "Slow and Steady" on page 3 to find out. As you read, remember to use the strategy Reread.

Quick Tip

If you read something you don't understand, stop and write or draw what you do not understand on a sticky note. Read the text again and look for context clues. Rereading may make the meaning clear. Use these sentence starters to help you.

- *I don't know . . .*
- *I reread that . . .*
- *Now I know that . . .*

Readers to Writers

An expository text tells readers about a topic. History lessons, science books, and biographies are examples of expository texts. The author presents a central idea and supports it with facts and evidence. The information in the text helps you to make inferences, or reach conclusions based on the evidence.

Diagrams and Headings

The selection "A World of Change" is an expository text. Expository text gives facts, examples, and explanations about a topic. It may include text features—such as diagrams, headings, or charts—that organize information.

FIND TEXT EVIDENCE

"A World of Change" is an expository text. It gives many facts about Earth's processes. Each section has a heading that tells me what the section is about. The diagram gives me more information on the topic.

Page 5

Like volcanic eruptions, landslides can happen without warning. They occur when rocks and dirt, loosened by heavy rains, slide down a hill or mountain. Some landslides are small. Others can be quite large and cause **severe** damage.

Cone Crater Vent Pipe Magma Chamber

Be Prepared

In contrast to slow-moving processes, people cannot prevent the effects of fast-moving natural disasters. Instead, scientists try to predict when these events will occur so that they can warn people. Still, some disasters are **unpredictable** and strike without warning. It is important for communities to have an emergency plan in place so that they can be evacuated quickly.

The surface of Earth constantly changes through natural processes. These processes can be gradual or swift. They help to make Earth the amazing planet that it is!

Summarize

Use your notes, the diagram, and the images to help you summarize "A World of Change." Compare slow and fast changes to Earth's surface.

Diagrams Diagrams show the parts of something or the way a process works. They have labels for their different parts.

Headings Headings tell what a section of text is mostly about.

COLLABORATE

Your Turn List three text features in "A World of Change." Tell your partner what information you learned from each of the features.

_____

_____

_____

_____

Compare and Contrast

Authors use text structure to organize the information in a text. Comparison is one kind of text structure. Authors who use this text structure tell how things are alike and different.

🔍 FIND TEXT EVIDENCE

Looking back at pages 3–4 of "A World of Change," I can reread to learn how slow natural processes and fast natural processes are alike and different. Words such as some, but, both, *and* like *let me know that a comparison is being made.*

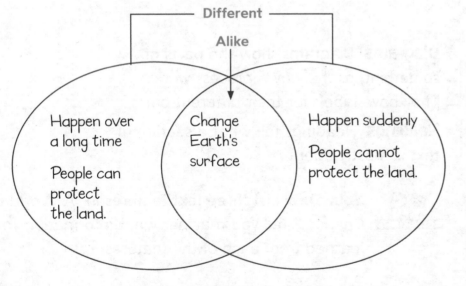

Different

Alike

Happen over a long time

People can protect the land.

Change Earth's surface

Happen suddenly

People cannot protect the land.

Your Turn Reread the section "Fast and Powerful" on pages 4–5. Compare and contrast <u>volcanoes</u> <u>and landslides</u>. List the information in the graphic organizer.

Westend61/Getty Images

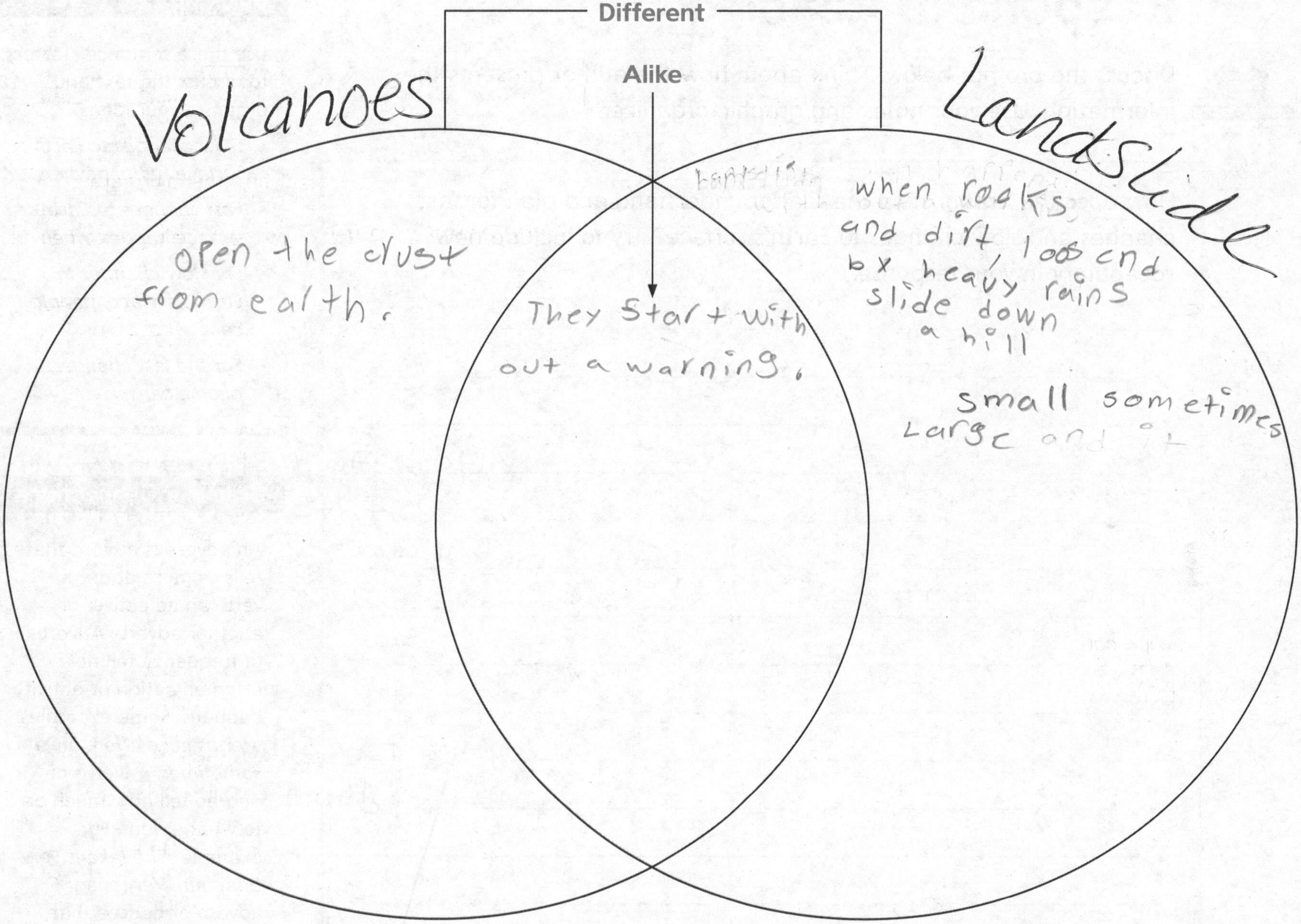

Different

Alike

Volcanoes

Landslide

open the crust from earth.

landslide

when rocks, and dirt, loose and by heavy rains slide down a hill

small sometimes large and it

They start with out a warning.

Respond to Reading

COLLABORATE

Discuss the prompt below. Think about how the author presents the information. Use your notes and graphic organizer.

How does the author help the reader understand and plan for fast changes and slow changes to Earth's surface? Try to include new vocabulary in your response.

_____

_____

_____

_____

_____

_____

_____

_____

_____

_____

_____

Quick Tip

Use these sentence starters to discuss the text and organize your ideas.

• *Slow changes to Earth's surface happen when . . .*

• *Fast changes to Earth's surface happen when . . .*

• *For slow changes to Earth's surface, people can . . .*

• *For the fast changes, people can... . . .*

Grammar Connections

An adverb is a word that tells us more about a verb, an adjective, or another adverb. Adverbs of frequency tell how often an action or activity happens. Some examples are: *usually, often, always, sometimes.* Adverbs of degree tell how much or to what extent. For example: *The lake is <u>very</u> beautiful. Very* is an adverb of degree that modifies the adjective *beautiful.*

Directions

Directions are step-by-step instructions for doing something. Read through all the steps before you begin a task. Then gather the materials you will need. Do each step in order. With your partner, read aloud and follow the directions below for a wind erosion experiment.

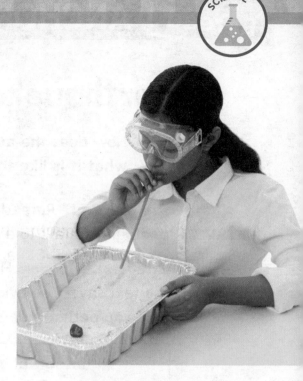

What You Need

- safety goggles
- 1 to 2 cups of sand
- 1 rectangular foil pan
- drinking straw
- markers and paper

Directions

1. Wear safety goggles.
2. Pour sand into the pan.
3. Spread sand to cover the bottom of the pan.
4. Use the straw to blow lightly across the top of the sand.
5. Observe and draw what happens.

What do you predict will happen when you blow on the sand? Write your prediction here.

_____

_____

_____

_____

Write Directions Research erosion with your partner. Find another experiment to show how erosion works. Your science book may have one. Then write your directions for the experiment. Be sure to

- include all the materials needed
- list the steps in order
- test the experiment to make sure it works

Restate the directions to your partner to make sure you haven't missed a step. Add photos and art to your directions. After you finish, you will be sharing your work with the class.

Ken Karp/McGraw-Hill Education

Earthquakes

How does the author use photographs to help you understand what it is like to live through an earthquake?

Literature Anthology: pages 10–19

COLLABORATE

Talk About It Reread **Literature Anthology** page 11 and look at the photograph. Talk to a partner about what you see in the photograph.

Cite Text Evidence How does the photograph help you understand what the text says? Use evidence from the text to explain how photographs help you better understand the text.

Photograph Clues	Text Evidence

Write The author uses a photograph to help me understand earthquakes by _____

_____

NigelSpiers/Shutterstock.com

Synthesize Information

When you synthesize information, you make conclusions based on your own knowledge and new information you learn from a text. Combine what you already know about how Earth's surface changes during fast and slow natural processes. How do earthquakes and weathering each change the Earth's surface?

? **How is Dr. Cifuentes' account of the earthquake different from the information in the rest of the selection?**

Talk About It Reread **Literature Anthology** page 13. Turn to a partner and talk about how Dr. Cifuentes describes what it felt like to live through an earthquake.

Cite Text Evidence What words and phrases describe what happens during and after an earthquake? Use this chart to record text evidence.

Dr. Cifuentes' Description	What I Learned

Write Dr. Cifuentes' account helps me understand _____

_____

_____

Make Inferences

An inference is a conclusion you make based on the facts presented in a text. When you reread the text, you can carefully gather evidence to help you make inferences. Then you can better explain and remember important ideas and details of the selection. Look at the map on page 12 of the Literature Anthology. What inference can you make about where the majority of earthquakes happen?

? How do you know that "Tsunami Terror" is a good heading for this section?

Quick Tip

When you reread, write down the descriptive words and phrases that the author uses. It will help you better understand tsunamis.

Talk About It Reread "Tsunami Terror" on pages 16–17 of the **Literature Anthology**. Turn to a partner and talk about how the author uses words to paint a picture of a tsunami.

Cite Text Evidence What words and phrases show that "Tsunami Terror" is a good heading for this section? Write text evidence in the web.

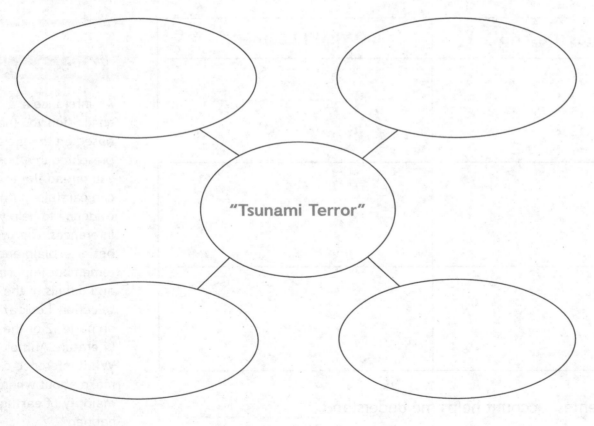

"Tsunami Terror"

Write "Tsunami Terror" is a good heading because _____

_____

Respond to Reading

Discuss the prompt below. Use your own knowledge about earthquakes to help you. Use your notes and graphic organizer.

How does the author use text features to help you understand how earthquakes affect people?

_____

_____

_____

_____

_____

_____

_____

_____

_____

_____

_____

_____

_____

Quick Tip

Use these sentence starters to organize your text evidence.

• *The author uses photographs with captions to show . . .*

• *The author includes a map and a diagram to show . . .*

• *The author also helps me understand earthquakes better by . . .*

• *I can see that earthquakes . . .*

Self-Selected Reading

Choose a text and fill in your writer's notebook with the title, author, and genre. Include a personal response to the text in your writer's notebook. To increase your understanding of the text, ask questions before and after you read. What might you learn about the topic? What else would you like to know?

Weathering the Storm

Literature Anthology
pages 22–23

1   I woke up at 5:00 a.m. to thunder and lightning. All morning it was pouring. All programs were canceled, which meant no horseback riding or tree climbing. Some of the troops had left that morning in case of flooding.

2   After lunch, I was walking to the bridge over the river. I looked at the field I had to cross and saw another river! Twenty-four hours earlier, the field had been dry. Our road was submerged, too. One thing was for sure: nobody was leaving our "island" anytime soon.

3   That night, a Brownie troop moved in with us. Their original cabin had been flooded through the chimney. There were tornado warnings that night, so to avoid more hazards, all of us kids piled into the bathroom to sleep.

Reread paragraph 2. **Draw a box** around the sentence that tells you a lot of rain fell in a short period of time.

Circle why the narrator says nobody was leaving the island anytime soon. Write the answer below.

nowbody could live because it was allready flooded.

COLLABORATE

Talk with a partner about how it is important for people to help each other during a natural disaster. **Underline** clues in paragraph 3 that tell how people helped each other.

[4] When morning came, we were a little sore and tired, but we were all fine. The same could not be said for the road out! The water level was even higher than before. We hesitated to call the EMS because they were busy taking care of real emergencies. We had plenty of food, water, and board games, so we were not in crisis.

[5] Some local troops left that day, taking the "emergency exit," an extremely muddy dirt road. But the problem of getting ourselves out remained. The main road was underwater, and the bridge would likely be ripped off by raging water. My mother's tiny car would never make it out on the muddy emergency exit road. We couldn't go on foot. We had to accept that we would have to stay another night and miss school and work.

Reread paragraph 4. **Underline** two reasons the Girl Scouts did not call EMS. Write the reasons in your own words here.

1 board games, so we were not in crisis.

2 we had plenty of food, water.

COLLABORATE

Look at the photograph and read the caption. Discuss why people may not be able to leave a flood area right away. **Circle** the sentences in paragraph 5 that tell why the narrator and others stayed another night.

The main road was underwater.

SPEED LIMIT 40

? How does the author order the events to help you understand what happens in a flood?

Talk About It Reread the excerpt on page 18. Talk with a partner about what happens at the camp.

Cite Text Evidence How does the author help you picture what a flood is and what it can do? Write text evidence in the chart.

First

↓

Next

↓

Then

↓

Last

Write I can understand what a flood is like because the author _____

_____

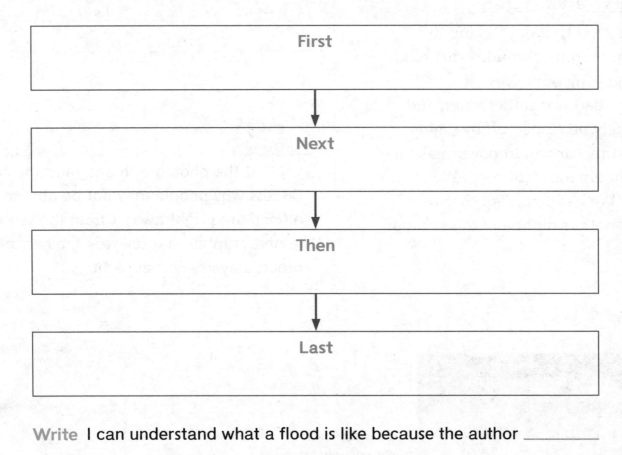

Author's Purpose

An **author's purpose** is the reason she or he writes something. It may be to inform, entertain, or persuade you to do something. Authors often use literal language (words that mean exactly what they say) when their purpose is to inform. They may use figurative language (such as hyperbole, simile, and metaphor) when their purpose is to entertain or persuade. Authors may use first-person point of view so readers can picture the author's experiences.

FIND TEXT EVIDENCE

On page 18 of "Weathering the Storm," the author gives information about the flood and how she responded to the flood. The author informs, but she also entertains by using humor in her personal narrative.

> After lunch, I was walking to the bridge over the river. I looked at the field I had to cross and saw another river! Twenty-four hours earlier, the field had been dry. Our road was submerged, too. One thing was for sure: nobody was leaving our "island" anytime soon.

Your Turn Reread paragraph 2 on page 18. What is the purpose of the last sentence? _____

_____

_____

Readers to Writers

Before you write, decide why you are writing—to inform, entertain, or persuade. In a personal narrative, you can write about a serious topic and still include experiences that were amusing. Use a combination of literal and figurative language in your writing.

Word Wise

Homophones are words that have the same pronunciation but different meanings or spellings: *not/knot, piece/peace, sun/son*. When writing, if you are not sure which word to use, look up the words' spellings in a dictionary. What homophones can you find in paragraph 2 on page 18?

Text Connections

? **How does the photographer show how rescue workers respond after a natural disaster? How does it compare to what you read in the "Masters of Disasters" Blast, *Earthquakes,* and "Weathering the Storm"?**

Talk About It Read the caption and look at the photograph. With a partner, talk about how the Coast Guard officer might feel about the devastation he sees from Hurricane Katrina. Talk about how you might feel.

Cite Text Evidence **Circle** clues in the photograph that show the effects of the hurricane. Then reread the caption and **underline** how technology helps people during natural disasters.

Write The photographer and authors help me understand how people respond to a natural disaster by

_____

_____

_____

_____

_____

_____

_____

A Coast Guard officer rides in a Jayhawk helicopter over New Orleans on August 30, 2005, after Hurricane Katrina. Helicopters helped responders find and rescue people trapped on rooftops following the devastating hurricane.

U.S. Coast Guard photograph by Petty Officer 2nd Class NyxoLyno Cangemi

SCIENCE

Present Your Work

COLLABORATE

Discuss how you and your partner will present your science experiment on erosion to the class. As you and your partner present the experiment, one person can give directions orally while the other follows them. Use the Presenting Checklist as you rehearse and give and get feedback.

Discuss the sentence starters below and write your answers.

The most interesting thing I learned about erosion is _____

_____

_____

I would like to plan another experiment to show _____

_____

_____

Oleksandr Koretskyi/Shutterstock.com

✓ Presenting Checklist

☐ Read the directions slowly and clearly.

☐ Keep eye contact with the audience as you do the experiment.

☐ Emphasize following the steps so the audience will be able to do your experiment, too.

☐ Listen carefully to questions from the audience.

☐ Answer any questions and listen to suggestions politely.

Expert Model

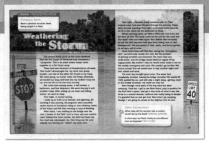

Literature Anthology: pages 22–23

Features of a Personal Narrative

A personal narrative is a nonfiction selection about an event in the author's life. A personal narrative

- gives facts, examples, and explanations about real people and events

- is told from the author's point of view—the first-person point of view—using words such as *I, me,* and *my*

- includes sensory details that support the main idea

- expresses the author's thoughts and feelings about an experience

Word Wise

On page 22, the author uses the informal phrase "One thing was <u>for sure</u>," instead of a more formal phrase, such as "One thing was <u>certain</u>." Using informal language helps to give her writing a friendly tone, or voice.

Analyze an Expert Model Reading personal narratives will help you learn how to write one. **Reread** page 22 of "Weathering the Storm" in the **Literature Anthology.** Write your answers below.

How does the author use sensory details?

_____

_____

List three examples of words or phrases the author uses to show the

sequence of events. _____

_____

_____

Plan: Choose Your Topic

Free Write Think about the times in your life when you tried your hardest to do something. On a separate sheet of paper, quickly write down your ideas for five minutes without stopping. Do not worry about spelling, grammar, or punctuation. Then exchange papers with a partner and discuss each other's ideas.

Writing Prompt Choose one idea that you want to expand into a personal narrative. What was the experience? Why was it hard for you?

I will write about _____

_____

_____

Purpose and Audience An **author's purpose** is his or her main reason for writing. What is your purpose for writing your personal narrative?

My purpose is to _____

_____

Think about the audience for your personal narrative. Who will read it?

My audience will be _____

I will use _____ tone when I write my personal narrative.

Plan In your writer's notebook, make a Sequence Chart like the one on the right to plan your writing.

Quick Tip

When you free write, you want to put all of your thoughts and ideas on paper as quickly as possible. These sentence starters will help you.

- *I remember when I . . .*
- *The hardest part was . . .*
- *I felt that . . .*

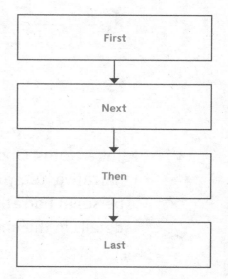

| First |
| Next |
| Then |
| Last |

Plan: Sequence

Put Events in Order Text structure is a way for writers to organize and present information. Most personal narratives have a sequential text structure. **Sequence** is the order in which things happen. Words and phrases such as *first, earlier, then, before, after, later,* and *last* signal the passage of time. As you reflect on the events in your personal narrative, answer these questions.

- How, when, and where does this event begin?
- What happens in the middle to show you are trying hard?
- How do you feel as these events happen?
- What happens at the end to show what you learned?

List two things you will tell about in the sequence of your narrative.

1 _____

_____

2 _____

_____

Take Notes Once you know the topic for your narrative, use your Sequence Chart to map out your personal narrative. Include only the most important details in the chart.

Draft

Sensory Details The author of a personal narrative uses **sensory details** to help readers see, hear, smell, taste, and feel what he or she did. In the example below from "Weathering the Storm," the author describes what she saw and how she felt so that readers can see and feel the same.

> Even though some parts of the trip were less than amazing, I had fun. I got to see flash floods, play in puddles for the first time in years, and get a tiny taste of what it was like to be in a natural disaster—without ever really being in danger. I'm grateful that no one got hurt. Next time I go camping, though, I am going to cancel at the slightest hint of rain!

Now use the above paragraph as a model to write about the time you tried hard to do something. Remember to use sensory words to help readers experience what you did.

_____

_____

_____

_____

Write a Draft Use your Sequence Chart to help you write your draft in your writer's notebook. Don't forget to link your ideas with sequence words to help your audience understand the order in which things happen.

Word Wise

Writers often use similes or metaphors to make comparisons so readers can picture what is happening. For example, a writer might compare the sound of a bouncing ball to a heartbeat. Or a writer might compare the feel of a leaf to soft silk. These comparisons help readers picture what the writer saw, heard, and felt in the story.

Revise

Strong Conclusion Effective personal narratives have strong, satisfying conclusions that support the purpose for writing. Some writers end with a memory, a feeling, or a hope. Other writers may end by circling back to remind readers of the introduction. Read the paragraph below. Then revise the last sentence to make a strong conclusion.

> Last fall I decided to try out for the school basketball team. I knew I needed to practice every day to be good enough to make the team. Practicing for hours every day wasn't easy. I remember one day my arms and legs ached from jumping and shooting baskets all morning. But I was determined to keep trying. It took all fall, but by the winter tryouts, I could shoot a free throw and make a basket almost every time. I'm sure that's what helped me make the team.

Grammar Connections

As you revise your draft, make sure you vary your sentence length and structure. For example, you don't want all your sentences to be short. Try combining some short sentences to make a few longer sentences. Remember, when you combine sentences, you can use a comma and a coordinating conjunction (*and, but, or, so, for, nor, yet*). For example: *I worked hard at tryouts, and I made the team!* You can also vary your sentences by beginning some sentences with a verb. For example: *Practice hard!*

_____

_____

_____

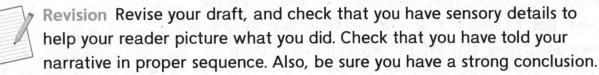

Revision Revise your draft, and check that you have sensory details to help your reader picture what you did. Check that you have told your narrative in proper sequence. Also, be sure you have a strong conclusion.

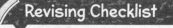
Peer Conferences

Review a Draft Listen actively as a partner reads his or her work aloud. Take notes about what you liked and what was difficult to follow. Begin by telling what you liked about the draft. Ask questions about the writing to clarify information. Make suggestions you think will make the writing more focused and coherent. Use these sentence starters:

Your beginning makes me want to read more because . . .

The sequence words you used help me . . .

This part is unclear to me. Can you explain how . . .?

I think your ending might be stronger if you . . .

Partner Feedback After your partner gives you feedback on your draft, write one of the suggestions that you will use in your revision. Refer to the rubric on page 31 as you give feedback.

Based on my partner's feedback, I will _____

_____

After you finish giving each other feedback, reflect on the peer conference. What was helpful? What might you do differently next time?

Revision As you revise your draft, use the Revising Checklist to help you figure out what ideas you may need to add, delete, combine, or rearrange. Remember to use the rubric on page 31 to help with your revision.

Revising Checklist

- [ ] Does the beginning of my personal narrative get the reader's attention and tell when and where the event happened?
- [ ] Did I use sequence words to organize the events?
- [ ] Did I use sensory details to help readers picture what happened?
- [ ] Does the conclusion tell how I feel about the experience?

Edit and Proofread

When you **edit** and **proofread** your writing, you look for and correct mistakes in spelling, punctuation, capitalization, and grammar. Reading through a revised draft multiple times can help you make sure you're catching any errors. Use the checklist below to edit your sentences.

✓ Editing Checklist

- ☐ Do all sentences begin with a capital letter and end with a punctuation mark?
- ☐ Are quotation marks used correctly?
- ☐ Does every sentence have a subject and verb?
- ☐ Do I use commas correctly in compound sentences?
- ☐ Are any multiple-meaning words used correctly?
- ☐ Are all words spelled correctly?

List two mistakes you found as you proofread your personal narrative.

1 _____

_____

2 _____

_____

Tech Tip

Grammar checkers are useful tools in word-processing programs. If the grammar checker identifies a sentence or phrase that is incorrect, use your checklist and ask yourself: Did I use the correct end punctuation? Did I use complete sentences? Am I missing a subject or a verb? Did I use multiple-meaning words correctly?

Grammar Connections

As you edit your draft, check verb tenses and the spelling of irregular verbs. Remember, a present-tense verb shows action happening now: *Today, I am playing with the team.* A past-tense verb shows action that already happened: *Yesterday, I went to tryouts.* A future-tense verb shows action that will happen: *Tomorrow, our team will play its first game!*

Publish, Present, and Evaluate

Publishing When you **publish** your writing, you create a neat final copy free of errors. Write your final draft legibly in cursive. Check that you are holding your pencil correctly between your forefinger and thumb.

Presentation When you are ready to **present** your work, rehearse your presentation. Use the Presenting Checklist to help you.

Evaluate After you publish your writing, use the rubric below to **evaluate** your writing.

What did you do successfully? _____

What needs more work? _____

_____

Presenting Checklist

- ☐ Stand or sit up straight and smile.
- ☐ Look at the audience.
- ☐ Speak clearly and with expression.
- ☐ Gesture as you read sensory words to help listeners visualize.
- ☐ Answer questions thoughtfully using details from your narrative.

4	3	2	1
• develops an engaging personal experience with sensory details • has a beginning, a middle, and an end with sequence words to tell events in order • has a strong conclusion that supports the rest of the story • is free or almost free of errors	• tells about a personal experience with some sensory details • has a beginning, a middle, and an end with some sequence words to link events in order • has a somewhat strong conclusion • has a few errors but is easy to read	• tries to describe a personal experience but lacks details • does not use sequence words and tells some events out of order • has a weak conclusion • has frequent errors that make it hard to understand	• does not share a personal experience and has no sensory details • tells events out of order and is confusing • does not have a conclusion • has many errors that make it difficult to follow

Talk About It

Essential Question

How do your actions affect others?

COLLABORATE

Have you ever heard the saying "Actions speak louder than words"? A broken promise is one example of actions speaking louder than words. Can you name another example?

How would you feel if you sat next to the two girls in the photograph?

List some of your actions and the effects they have had on the people around you. Then talk with a partner about how your actions can affect others.

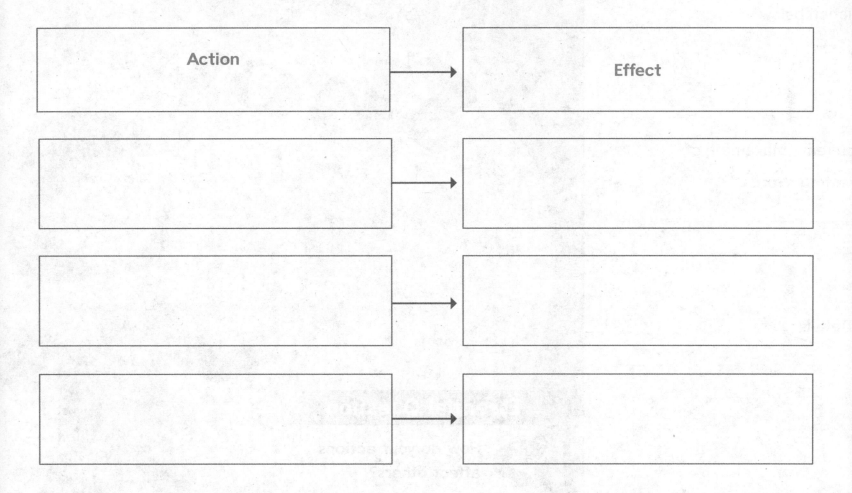

Action	Effect

BLAST BACK!
studysync

Go online to **my.mheducation.com** and read the "Friends Forever" Blast. Think about the friendships you have read about in stories. What qualities does a good friend have? Then blast back your response.

Masterfile

TAKE NOTES

To help you focus as you read, preview the story and the illustrations. What do you think the story will be about? Write your prediction below.

_____

_____

_____

As you read, make note of:

Interesting Words _____

_____

_____

Key Details _____

_____

_____

_____

_____

_____

THE Talent Show

Essential Question

? **How do your actions affect others?**

Read about how Tina's actions affect Maura.

"Tina, there's a school talent show in three weeks," I shouted to my best friend. My older brother had been teaching me juggling, and I knew he'd help me with my act for the show.

Tina ran over to the bulletin board and read the poster. "Maura, what's our act going to be?" Tina asked me.

"Our act?" I said, taking a tighter grip on my books.

Tina grinned, pointed to the poster and said, "It says acts can be individuals, partners, or small groups."

My grip on my books became **uncomfortably** tight. "You want to do an act together?"

"It'll be fun," Tina said.

I **hesitated** for a second before continuing. "I've got an idea and . . ."

Tina interrupted me. "Yeah, me too; let's talk at lunch."

During math, I tried to think of how I would tell Tina that I wanted to do my own act. After all, we are best friends; we should be able to see eye to eye about this. The problem is Tina always takes charge, I don't speak up, and then I end up feeling resentful about the whole situation.

I **desperately** wanted to win, but it was more than that. I wanted to win on my own—with an act that was all mine.

FIND TEXT EVIDENCE

Read

Paragraphs 1–8
Dialogue

Circle the dialogue that shows that Tina likes to take charge. What word would you use to describe Tina's behavior?

_____

_____

Paragraphs 9-10
Problem and Solution

Underline the problem that Maura faces. What inference can you make about Maura?

_____

_____

_____

Reread

Author's Craft

How does the author's word choice help you predict how Maura might solve the problem?

FIND TEXT EVIDENCE 🔍

Read

Paragraphs 1–4
Idioms

Circle the words in paragraph 4 that help you understand the meaning of the idiom *to let off steam*.

Paragraphs 5–8
Make Predictions

What does Maura's grandmother say to encourage Maura to speak up for herself? **Draw a box** around the text evidence. Write what you predict will happen next.

_____

_____

_____

_____

Reread

Author's Craft

How does the author use the character of Maura's grandmother to help Maura solve her problem?

At lunch, Tina started talking as soon as we sat down. "I have it all planned out. My **inspiration** came from that new TV show, *You've Got Talent*. We can sing along to a song and do a dance routine, and my mother can make us costumes."

"Yeah, that's good," I said. "But I had another idea." I told her about my juggling act.

Tina considered it. "Nah, I don't think I can learn to juggle in three weeks and I'd probably drop the balls," she said. "We don't want to be **humiliated**, right?"

At recess, I ran around the track a couple of times just to let off steam.

When my grandmother picked me up after school, she drove a few minutes and finally said, "Cat got your tongue?"

I explained about the talent show as she listened carefully. "So, Tina is not being respectful of your ideas, but it sounds as if you aren't either."

"What?" I shouted. "I told Tina her idea was good."

"No," said my grandmother, "I said that you weren't respectful of your own ideas, or you would have spoken up. I understand that you're friends, but you're still **accountable** for your own actions."

I thought about this. "So what should I do?" I asked.

"I **advise** you to tell the truth," she said. "It wouldn't hurt to let Tina know what you want. Besides," my grandmother added, "it will be good for your **self-esteem**!"

When we got home, I took 12 deep breaths, called Tina, and told her that I was going to do my juggling act. She was curt on the phone, and I spent all night worrying she would be mad at me.

The next day, she described her act and her costume. But the biggest surprise came at recess, when we played a game that I chose, not Tina.

I guess standing up for myself did pay off.

Summarize

Use your notes to write a summary of what happened in "The Talent Show." Talk about whether your prediction on page 34 was confirmed.

FIND TEXT EVIDENCE

Read

Paragraphs 1–5

Problem and Solution

Circle the dialogue that helps Maura think about how to solve her problem. What does Maura's grandmother want her to do?

_____

_____

Dialogue

Underline the text that is part of the rising action. A rising action is an event or decision that causes a change that leads to a climax.

Synthesize Information

How do Maura's actions affect Tina by the end of the story?

Reread

Author's Craft

How does the author show how Maura feels after she stands up for herself?

Vocabulary

Use the example sentences to talk with a partner about each word. Then answer the questions.

accountable

Sami is held **accountable** when he forgets to walk his dog.

How are the words *accountable* and *responsible* similar?

_____

_____

advise

A coach can **advise** you on how to improve your swimming.

What is a synonym for *advise?*

_____

_____

desperately

The man tried **desperately** to remember where he parked the car.

Describe a time when you tried desperately to remember something.

_____

_____

hesitated

The cat **hesitated** before jumping off the table.

When have you hesitated before doing something?

_____

_____

humiliated

Isabel felt **humiliated** when she forgot her homework.

How is *humiliated* similar to *embarrassed?*

_____

_____

Build Your Word List Reread the third paragraph on page 37. Circle the word *curt.* Use a print or online dictionary to find the word's meaning, syllabication, and pronunciation. Write the meaning in your writer's notebook.

inspiration

The artist found **inspiration** in nature for her painting.

When you have to write a story, what gives you inspiration?

_____

_____

self-esteem

Scoring a goal in the game helped improve Billy's confidence and **self-esteem**.

What else builds self-esteem?

_____

_____

uncomfortably

Sonya's throat felt **uncomfortably** sore.

What are some things that can feel uncomfortably tight?

_____

_____

Idioms

Idioms are phrases that have a meaning different from the meaning of each word in the phrase. Sometimes context clues can help you figure out the meaning of an idiom.

🔍 FIND TEXT EVIDENCE

When I read the idiom see eye to eye _on page 35 in "The Talent Show," the words_ After all, we are best friends _help me figure out its meaning._ To see eye to eye _means "to agree."_

After all, we are best friends; we should be able to see eye to eye about this.

Your Turn Use context clues to help you figure out the meanings of the following idioms. Use an online resource to check your work.

cat got your tongue, page 36 _____

_____

standing up for myself, page 37 _____

_____

Make Predictions

When you read, use story details to make predictions about what will happen. As you read "The Talent Show," make predictions.

🔍 **FIND TEXT EVIDENCE**

You probably predicted Tina is the kind of friend who is bossy. Reread page 35 of the story to find the text evidence that confirms your prediction.

Page 35

During math, I tried to think of how I would tell Tina that I wanted to do my own act. After all, we are best friends; we should be able to see eye to eye about this. The problem is Tina always takes charge. I don't speak up, and then I end up feeling resentful about the whole situation.

I read that Tina always takes charge. This confirms my prediction that Tina is bossy.

Your Turn Using clues you find in the text, how do you predict Maura will solve a future problem with her friends? As you read, use the strategy Make Predictions.

_____

_____

_____

Dialogue

The selection "The Talent Show" is **realistic fiction**. Realistic fiction is a made-up story that has characters, settings, and events that could happen in real life. It usually has dialogue. Realistic fiction has a plot that usually includes a rising action, climax, falling action, and resolution.

🔍 FIND TEXT EVIDENCE

I can tell that "The Talent Show" is realistic fiction. The story mostly takes place at school. The dialogue between Maura and Tina is realistic. They act and speak like people who might go to my school.

Readers to Writers

Writers use dialogue to help their readers learn more about the characters in a story. Dialogue helps readers understand how the characters feel and the changes they go through. How can you use dialogue in your own writing?

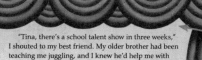

Page 35

"Tina, there's a school talent show in three weeks," I shouted to my best friend. My older brother had been teaching me juggling, and I knew he'd help me with my act for the show.

Tina ran over to the bulletin board and read the poster. "Maura, what's our act going to be?" Tina asked me.

"Our act?" I said, taking a tighter grip on my books.

Tina grinned, pointed to the poster and said, "It says acts can be individuals, partners, or small groups."

My grip on my books became **uncomfortably** tight. "You want to do an act together?"

"It'll be fun," Tina said.

I **hesitated** for a second before continuing. "I've got an idea and . . ."

Tina interrupted me. "Yeah, me too; let's talk at lunch."

During math, I tried to think of how I would tell Tina that I wanted to do my own act. After all, we are best friends; we should be able to see eye to eye about this. The problem is Tina always takes charge, I don't speak up, and then I end up feeling resentful about the whole situation.

I **desperately** wanted to win, but it was more than that. I wanted to win on my own—with an act that was all mine.

Dialogue Dialogue is the exact words the characters say.

Your Turn With a partner, identify dialogue from "The Talent Show" that shows Tina likes to take charge.

_____

_____

_____

Problem and Solution

The main character in a story often has a **problem** that needs to be solved. The steps the character takes to find a **solution** to the problem make up the story's events, or the plot of the story.

🔍 FIND TEXT EVIDENCE

As I reread pages 35 and 36 of "The Talent Show," I can see that Maura has a problem. I will list the events in the story. Then I can figure out how Maura finds a solution.

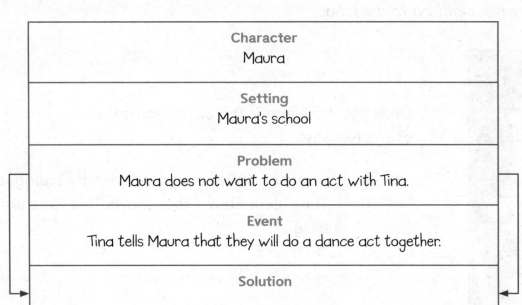

Character Maura
Setting Maura's school
Problem Maura does not want to do an act with Tina.
Event Tina tells Maura that they will do a dance act together.
Solution

 Your Turn Reread "The Talent Show." Find other story events. Use these events to identify the solution and list them in the graphic organizer on page 43.

Quick Tip

The plot has a rising action, climax, falling action, and resolution. The rising action is the story events that describe the character's problem. The climax is the turning point of the story or when things start to move in a different direction. The falling action is the story events where the problem starts to get solved. And the resolution is the solution to the problem. Reread and look for the events that help Maura solve her problem.

Character
Setting
Problem
Event
Solution

Respond to Reading

COLLABORATE

Discuss the prompt below. Think about how the author presents Maura's problem and solution. Use your notes and graphic organizer.

How does the author organize the story events to show the rising action, climax, falling action, and solution?

_____

_____

_____

_____

_____

_____

_____

_____

_____

_____

_____

_____

Quick Tip

Use the following sentence starters to describe the story events.

- *A story event that describes a rising action is . . .*

- *The story event that is the climax is when Maura . . .*

- *A story event that describes a falling action is when Tina . . .*

- *The resolution is when Maura . . .*

Grammar Connections

As you write your response, be sure to put any dialogue that you pick up from the story in quotation marks. Remember that the end punctuation goes inside the end quotation mark.

Maura says, "Our act?"

Tina tells her, "But I had another idea."

Business Letter

You write a **business letter** when you want to contact someone in a business, organization, or government. It is formal in format, tone, and writing style. Business letters can request information, ask for help, or tell someone about a problem. A business letter includes the date, address, greeting, body, complimentary close, and signature.

Where have you seen a business letter before? Write your answer.

_____

Write a Business Letter With a partner, write a business letter to a state representative about a state law.

- Identify a law in your state that you want to learn more about.
- Ask your teacher or an adult to help you research the name and address of one of your state representatives online.
- Write a business letter to ask for more information about the law. You may also share your opinion about the law.

If you share your opinion in your business letter, you should say what you do or do not like about the law, and how you think it should be changed. After you finish, you will be sharing your work with the class.

Wilton Q. Furmani
1234 Canyon Drive
Central City, AW 00000

May 1, 2018

Ms. Viola Smart, President
Acme Corporation
100 Roadrunner Way
Central City, AZ 00000

Dear Ms. Smart:

I am a customer. I recently received your catalog and saw that you stopped selling trampolines. I need a new one and wanted to order it from your company. Will you be selling trampolines again in the future? If not, I wonder if you can tell me how to reach the manufacturer.

Thank you so much for your assistance on this matter.

Sincerely,

Wilton Q. Furmani
Wilton Q. Furmani

The example above shows a business letter. **Circle** the greeting. Who is the writer of the letter? Write your answer below.

_____

_____

_____

Experts, Incorporated

Literature Anthology: pages 24–33

? **How does the author use dialogue to make the characters seem like people you might know in real life?**

COLLABORATE

Talk About It Reread the dialogue on page 25 of the **Literature Anthology**. Does the author do a good job using realistic dialogue between Rodney and his friends? Turn to your partner and talk about whether you agree or not.

Cite Text Evidence Find examples of realistic dialogue and write them in the chart. Write text evidence and explain if the dialogue is effective.

Evaluate Information

Think about the way you speak. Compare it to the dialogue in the text. Which words sound similar to the words you use? Is the author's use of dialogue realistic?

Dialogue	Is it effective?

Write The characters sound like people I might know because the author _____

_____

_____

? **How does the author build tension when Rodney tries to think of what to write about?**

Talk About It Reread the third paragraph on page 29 in the **Literature Anthology**. Turn to a partner and talk about how the author describes what Rodney is thinking.

Cite Text Evidence How does the author help you understand how Rodney feels as he tries to think of an idea? Write clues in the web.

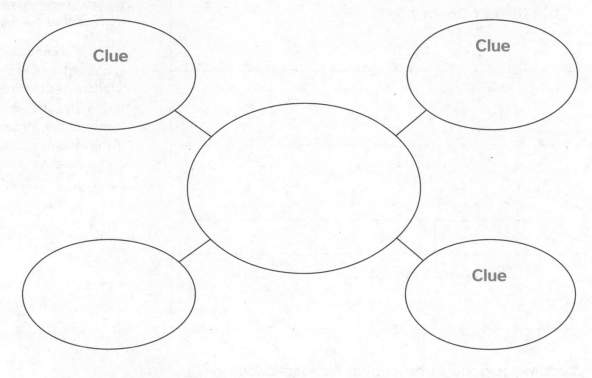

Clue

Clue

Clue

Write The author builds tension by _____

_____

_____

? **How do you know that Rodney is good at defending and describing his idea to others?**

Talk About It Reread page 31. Talk with a partner about how Lucas reacts to Rodney's idea.

Cite Text Evidence How does Rodney convince Lucas that his idea is a good one? Write text evidence in the chart below.

What Rodney Says

↓

What Lucas Thinks

Write I know that Rodney is good at describing his idea because _____

_____

_____

Quick Tip

The parts of the story where Rodney is speaking directly to the reader can help you understand what he is thinking and how he is feeling.

Synthesize Information

Think about how the character of Rodney addresses the reader directly, and what he tells the reader. What does that tell you about his character?

Respond to Reading

COLLABORATE

Discuss the prompt below. Apply your own experience with problems and finding solutions to inform your answer. Use your notes and graphic organizer.

How does the author use dialogue to help you understand how Rodney feels as he struggles and then comes up with an idea?

_____

_____

_____

_____

_____

_____

_____

_____

_____

_____

_____

_____

_____

_____

Quick Tip

Use these sentence starters to organize your text evidence.

- *Sarah Weeks uses dialogue to show that Rodney and his friends. . .*
- *The dialogue helps me understand. . .*
- *The author also uses dialogue to show that Rodney can. . .*

Self-Selected Reading

Choose a text. Read the first two pages. If five or more words are unfamiliar, pick another text. Fill in your writer's notebook with the title, author, genre, and your purpose for reading.

Speaking Out to Stop Bullying

Literature Anthology:
pages 36–39

Communities Take a Stand

1   New Hampshire passed a law to stop bullies. The law states that all school staff must be trained to know what bullying looks like. People learn to spot the signs of bullying. The law tells people who see bullying to report it. The state hopes that the law will create bully-free schools.

2   In Midland, Texas, the police take their message to the schools. Police officers make sure to tell students that bullying can be a crime. They want bullies to know that they are accountable for what they do. This means that bullies will be punished if they are caught. The officers tell students who have been bullied or who have seen bullying to report it right away. They make it clear that people have choices. They tell students that anyone can choose to stop being a bully.

Reread paragraph 1. **Circle** the sentences that describe the law New Hampshire has about bullying. Write the sentences below.

_____

_____

_____

_____

_____

COLLABORATE

Reread paragraph 2. Talk with a partner about the message police officers take to schools. **Underline** the three sentences that police officers tell students about bullying.

Young People Speak Out

[3] . . . Actress Lauren Potter has a message for lawmakers. She has been speaking out about the bullying of special-needs students. Lauren was born with Down Syndrome. Because she did not look like her classmates, she was teased and called names as a child. She wants laws that will keep people safe from bullies.

Learning to Speak Up

[4] It is important for people everywhere to recognize and stand up to bullying. Everyone has a right to feel safe and to be treated with respect. Likewise, each person has a responsibility to treat others with respect. Report anything that may get in the way of maintaining a safe environment.

Reread paragraph 3. **Underline** the sentence that tells what Lauren Potter speaks out about to lawmakers.

COLLABORATE

Reread paragraph 4. Talk with a partner about what the author is saying you can do to stop bullying. **Draw a box** around the sentence that supports your response. Write the sentence below.

_____

_____

_____

How do you know how the author feels about bullying?

Talk About It Look back at the excerpts on pages 50 and 51. Talk about how the author feels about bullying.

Cite Text Evidence What clues help you understand the author's feelings about bullying? Write text evidence here.

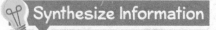 **Synthesize Information**

When you reread, think about how you feel about bullying and compare your feelings to the author's feelings. If you're not sure how the author feels, the author's choice of words can help you figure out how he feels.

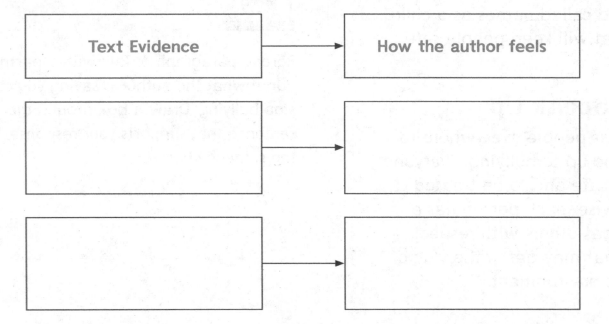

Text Evidence	→	How the author feels
	→	
	→	

Write The author helps me understand how he feels about bullying by

_____

_____

_____

Fact and Opinion

Quick Tip

To find out if a sentence is a fact or opinion, use these questions: *Can this be proven true or false?* If yes, it is a fact. *Is this how someone feels or thinks?* If yes, this is an opinion.

Facts are statements that can be proven true or false. *The United States of America is a country in North America.* That's a fact. You can research the statement and prove it is true. **Opinions** can't be proven; they are an author's personal beliefs or judgments. You might agree or disagree with them. *Driving is the best way to see the United States.* That's an opinion.

FIND TEXT EVIDENCE

On page 37 of "Speaking Out to Stop Bullying," the author states an opinion in the first sentence. By telling us that bullying is one of the toughest issues facing students today, the author believes bullying is an important topic. The next sentence is a fact: "Bullying occurs when a person uses aggressive behavior to hurt others on purpose." It can be proven true by looking up the word *bullying* in a dictionary.

> One of the toughest issues facing students today is bullying.
> **Bullying occurs when a person uses aggressive behavior to hurt others on purpose.**

Your Turn Reread page 51.

- What is a fact the author tells you about Lauren Potter?

_____

- What is the author's opinion about learning to speak up?

_____

Text Connections

? **How do the girls in the photograph below and the authors of *Experts Incorporated* and "Speaking Out to Stop Bullying" help you understand how your actions might affect others?**

Talk About It Read the caption and look at the photograph. Talk with a partner about what the girls are doing.

Cite Text Evidence What clues help you see how the older girl is affecting the life of the younger girl? **Circle** them in the photograph. Reread the caption and **underline** text evidence that tells why the two girls are together.

Write The photograph and the authors help me understand how my actions could affect others by _____

_____

_____

_____

_____

_____

The two girls are both part of a program in their community that teams older students with younger ones. The younger girl is learning to play baseball.

When you read, use clues in photographs and illustrations to help you better understand the text. For example, look at the actions of the people. The expressions on their faces can tell you how they feel.

Quick Tip

SOCIAL STUDIES

Present Your Work

COLLABORATE

Discuss how you will present your business letter to the class and how you will send it to the state representative after you have presented it. Use the Listening Checklist as you listen to your classmates' presentations. Complete the sentences below.

An interesting fact I learned about the law is _____

_____

_____

I would like to know more about _____

_____

_____

_____

✓ **Listening Checklist**

☐ Pay attention to how the speaker uses visuals.

☐ Listen to the speaker carefully.

☐ Take notes on what you liked about the presentation.

☐ Wait until after the presentation to comment on it.

☐ If someone else makes the same comment first, tell why you agree with him or her.

Tony Freeman/PhotoEdit

Talk About It

How do you start a business and help people at the same time? A woman in New York did it. She started a bakery that includes a culinary training program for immigrants. The training program has been successful, and the bakery's breads are a big hit, too.

How do you think starting a business can help a community? Write your ideas in the word web.

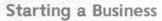

Starting a Business

Go online to **my.mheducation.com** and read the "Helping Others Is Good Business" Blast. Think about how these businesses help people and make money. Then blast back your response.

ESTABLISH A PURPOSE FOR READING

Understanding why you are reading helps you adjust how you read. If you are reading for information, you might reread sections to make sure you understand the text. Preview the text and write your purpose for reading.

_____

_____

_____

As you read, make note of:

Interesting Words _____

_____

_____

_____

Key Details _____

_____

_____

_____

Essential Question

How can starting a business help others?

Read about how two companies are making a difference.

Kwaku Alston/Stockland Martel

Dollars and $ENSE

Behind the success of these big businesses is a desire to help others.

Good business is not always about the bottom line. A **compassionate** company knows that making money is not the only way to measure success. Many large businesses in the United States and all over the world are finding unusual ways to help people in need.

Hearts and Soles

After starting and running four businesses, Blake Mycoskie wanted a break from his usual **routine**. In 2006, he traveled to Argentina, in South America, and while he was there he learned to sail and to dance. He also visited poor villages where very few of the children had shoes. Mycoskie decided he had to do something. "I'm going to start a shoe company, and for every pair I sell, I'm going to give one pair to a kid in need."

For this inventive new **undertaking**, Mycoskie started the business using his own money. He named it TOMS: Shoes for Tomorrow. The slip-on shoes are modeled on shoes that are traditionally worn by Argentine workers.

Mycoskie immediately set up his **innovative** one-for-one program. TOMS gives away one pair of shoes for every pair that is purchased. Later that year, Mycoskie returned to Argentina and gave away 10,000 pairs of shoes. By 2016, TOMS had donated over 60 million pairs.

FIND TEXT EVIDENCE 🔍

Read

Paragraph 1
Main Idea and Details
Underline the main idea of the first paragraph.

Paragraphs 2–4
Reread
Circle the details that tell you what Mycoskie noticed when he visited villages in Argentina. What did this cause him to do?

Suffixes

The suffix -*ive* means "related or belonging to." **Draw a box** around the word in the third paragraph with the suffix -*ive*.

Reread
Author's Craft

What is the author's purpose for using "Sense" instead of "Cents" in the title "Dollars and Sense"?

FIND TEXT EVIDENCE 🔍

Read

Paragraphs 1–2
Reread

Circle the text evidence that shows what Mycoskie's company did next. What has this taught Mycoskie?

_____

_____

_____

Paragraphs 3–5
Main Idea and Details

Underline the detail that best explains one way Hard Rock Cafe raises money to give back to the community.

Reread
Author's Craft

How does the author's use of Blake Mycoskie's own words help support the author's claim that businesses can give back?

TOMS' employees unpack shoes to give away.

The company has expanded to sell eyeglasses. In a similar program, one pair of eyeglasses is donated for every pair that is bought.

Mycoskie is pleased and surprised. "I always thought I would spend the first half of my life making money and the second half giving it away," Mycoskie says. "I never thought I could do both at the same time."

Giving Back Rocks!

Have you ever seen a Hard Rock Cafe? The company runs restaurants and hotels. In 1990, the company launched a new **enterprise**: charity. Since then, it has given away millions of dollars to different causes. Its motto is Love All, Serve All.

One way the company raises **funds** for charity is by selling a line of T-shirts. The **process** starts with rock stars designing the art that goes on the shirts. Then the shirts are sold on the Internet. Part of the money that is raised from the sales of the shirts is given to charity.

Employees at Hard Rock Cafe locations are encouraged to raise money for their community. Every store does it differently.

Hard Rock Cafes are committed to giving back to the community.

(t) Kwaku Alston/Stockland Martel; (b) Thomas A. Kelly/Corbis/VCG/Getty Images

Top Five Charities

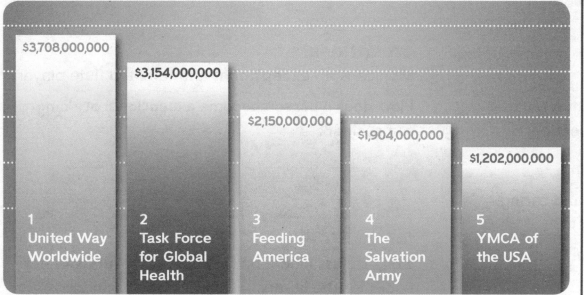

$3,708,000,000
1 United Way Worldwide

$3,154,000,000
2 Task Force for Global Health

$2,150,000,000
3 Feeding America

$1,904,000,000
4 The Salvation Army

$1,202,000,000
5 YMCA of the USA

Source: Forbes.com

Individuals as well as businesses are committed to helping people in need. This graph shows the American charities that got the most donations in 2016 and how much money they raised.

The restaurant in Hollywood, Florida, worked with some **exceptional** students from two Florida high schools. Together, they put on an event to raise money for the Make-A-Wish Foundation. The foundation grants wishes to children with serious medical problems.

The Bottom Line

Every day companies are thinking of innovative ways to give back to their community.

If you own a business, making a profit is a necessity. However, helping others is just as important as the bottom line. Helping others is good business!

> **Summarize**
>
> Identify the main idea of each section of "Dollars and Sense." Then use these main ideas to summarize the overall text.

ARGUMENTATIVE TEXT

FIND TEXT EVIDENCE 🔍

Read

Graphs and Headings

Underline the heading on the graph. Which charity donated the most in 2016? Write it below.

_____

Paragraphs 1–2

Main Idea and Details

Draw a box around the sentence that summarizes the main idea.

Reread

Author's Craft

The "bottom line" refers to profit a business makes. It also means the main idea of something. How does the play on words in the heading relate to the text?

Fluency

Take turns reading the last paragraph aloud to a partner. Pay attention to the punctuation marks. They will help you with the phrasing and rate as you read aloud.

Vocabulary

Use the example sentences to talk with a partner about each word. Then answer the questions.

compassionate

I could tell Milo was a **compassionate** and caring person by the way he hugged his brother.

What is an antonym for *compassionate*?

_____

_____

enterprise

Starting a white-water rafting business was an exciting new **enterprise** for Reynaldo.

What new enterprises are there in your community?

_____

_____

exceptional

Monica is an **exceptional** and talented flute player.

How does a person become exceptional at doing something?

_____

_____

funds

Elena's class held a bake sale to raise **funds** to buy books for the library.

What project would you like to raise funds for?

_____

_____

innovative

Ming enjoyed trying out the **innovative** new wheelchair.

What new technology do you think was innovative for its time?

_____

_____

Build Your Word List Underline a word in "Dollars and Sense" that you find interesting. Make a word web of different forms of the word. Use a print or online dictionary to look up the meanings of each word. Many online dictionaries let you listen to words' pronunciation and syllabication as well.

process

An important step in the **process** of making a pie is to roll out the crust.

What is one step in the process of baking cookies?

_____

_____

routine

Barak loved the daily **routine** of walking his dog.

Why is it helpful to have a morning routine?

_____

_____

undertaking

Cleaning up Tim's messy bedroom was going to be a big **undertaking**.

What would you consider a big undertaking?

_____

_____

Suffixes

A **suffix** is a word part added to the end of a word to change its meaning and often its part of speech. Look at the suffixes below.

-ly = "done in the way of"
-ive = "related or belonging to"
-ity = "state or quality of"

🔍 FIND TEXT EVIDENCE

I see the word innovative *on page 59 of "Dollars and Sense." Looking at its word parts, I see the base word* innovate. *The suffix* -ive *changes the verb* innovate *into an adjective. This suffix will help me figure out what* innovative *means.*

Mycoskie immediately set up his innovative one-for-one program.

Your Turn Use suffixes and context clues to figure out the meanings of the following words:

immediately, page 59 _____

traditionally, page 59 _____

necessity, page 61 _____

Reread

When you read an argumentative text, you may come across ideas and information that are new to you. As you read "Dollars and Sense," reread sections to make sure you understand the key facts and details in the text.

🔍 FIND TEXT EVIDENCE

As you read, you may want to make sure you understand the ways a business can help others. Reread the section "Hearts and Soles" in "Dollars and Sense."

Page 59

Mycoskie decided he had to do something. "I'm going to start a shoe company, and for every pair I sell, I'm going to give one pair to a kid in need."

I read that TOMS gives away one pair of shoes for every pair of shoes that someone buys. From this text evidence, I can draw the inference that the more shoes TOMS sells, the more shoes can be given away.

Your Turn What is another example of a company giving back to the community? Reread page 60 to answer the question. As you read other selections, remember to use the strategy Reread.

_____

_____

_____

Ariel Skelley/Blend Images

Graphs and Headings

"Dollars and Sense" is a persuasive article, a form of argumentative text. In this genre, the author states an opinion on the topic or makes a claim. To support the claim, the article provides facts and examples from trusted sources. A persuasive article is nonfiction. It may include text features, such as **graphs** and **headings**.

FIND TEXT EVIDENCE

"Dollars and Sense" states the author's opinion and tries to get readers to agree. It includes headings, as well as a graph that shows the amount of money raised by different charities.

Page 61

Top Five Charities

$3,708,000,000

$3,154,000,000

$2,150,000,000

$1,904,000,000

$1,202,000,000

| 1 United Way Worldwide | 2 Task Force for Global Health | 3 Feeding America | 4 The Salvation Army | 5 YMCA of the USA |

Source: Forbes.com

Individuals as well as businesses are committed to helping people in need. This graph shows the American charities that got the most donations in 2016 and how much money they raised.

The restaurant in Hollywood, Florida, worked with some **exceptional** students from two Florida high schools. Together, they put on an event to raise money for the Make-A-Wish Foundation. The foundation grants wishes to children with serious medical problems.

If you own a business, making a profit is a necessity. However, helping others is just as important as the bottom line. Helping others is good business!

Summarize

Identify the main idea of each section of "Dollars and Sense." Then use these main ideas to summarize the overall text.

The Bottom Line

Every day companies are thinking of innovative ways to give back to their community.

Graphs help you picture numerical information. This bar graph helps you compare information.

Headings tell you what the section is mostly about.

Your Turn Find and list two text features in "Dollars and Sense." Tell what information you learned from each of the features.

COLLABORATE

_____

_____

_____

Main Idea and Details

Quick Tip

To find the main idea, ask, "What is this text mostly about?" To find the key details, ask, "What important examples support this main idea?"

The **main idea** is the most important idea that an author presents in a text or a section of text. Key **details** give important information to support the main idea.

🔍 FIND TEXT EVIDENCE

When I reread the second paragraph in the section "Giving Back Rocks!" on page 60 of "Dollars and Sense," I can identify the key details. Next, I can evaluate what the details have in common. Then I can determine the main idea of the section.

Main Idea
Hard Rock Cafe sells a line of T-shirts to raise funds for charity.
Detail
Rock stars design the art that goes on the shirts.
Detail
The shirts are sold on the Internet.
Detail
Part of the money that is raised from the sales of the shirts is given to charity.

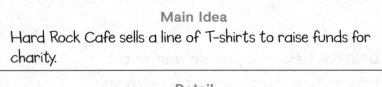

Your Turn Reread the section "Hearts and Soles" on pages 59–60 of "Dollars and Sense." Find the key details in the section and list them in your graphic organizer on page 67. Use the details to determine the main idea.

Main Idea
Detail
Detail
Detail

Respond to Reading

COLLABORATE

Discuss the prompt below. Think about the author's argument that businesses can make a profit and still help others. Use your notes and graphic organizer.

How does the author's use of text features help support the author's claim that businesses can help others and make a profit?

_____

_____

_____

_____

_____

_____

_____

_____

_____

_____

_____

_____

Quick Tip

Use these sentence starters to help you organize your text evidence.

- *The headings tell me . . .*
- *The photos show . . .*
- *The graph shows that . . .*
- *The caption tells . . .*

Grammar Connection

Remember to use the correct conjunction and punctuation to avoid run-on sentences. Notice that there are two complete sentences in the following example. *I walk my dog every morning, we go to the park.* Normally, you would end each sentence with a period. To connect the two independent clauses, the conjunction *and* must follow the comma. That will avoid a run-on sentence, called a comma splice.

Primary and Secondary Sources

Primary sources help us to learn about the past. A primary source may be an original document from the time being studied or an account by someone who witnessed an event. Examples of primary sources are

- photographs and maps
- letters and diary entries
- autobiographies

Secondary sources are created by someone who does not have firsthand knowledge of the topic. Secondary sources include magazine articles, encyclopedias, and documentaries.

What is another example of a secondary source? Write your answer.

_____

Create a Biographical Sketch With a partner or a group, choose an entrepreneur, or business leader, from your state. Write a biographical sketch about that person.

- Use both primary and secondary sources.
- Include photographs, slides, audio, and/or video to present your information.
- Make a bibliography, a list of all the sources you used.

Add slides or video to your biographical sketch. After you finish, you will be sharing your work with the class.

The image above shows two primary sources: an old photograph and a diary. Is an interview a primary or secondary source? Why?

_____

_____

_____

_____

_____

_____

_____

_____

_____

aurorat/iStock/Getty Images

Kids in Business

How does the author help you understand how he feels about young entrepreneurs?

Literature Anthology: pages 40–43

COLLABORATE

Talk About It Reread page 41 of the **Literature Anthology**. Turn to a partner and talk about Hayleigh's and Joshua's businesses.

Cite Text Evidence What phrases show how the author feels about what Hayleigh and Joshua are doing? Write text evidence in the chart.

Text Evidence	How the Author Feels

Make Inferences

Authors use specific words that give clues about how they feel about a topic. As you read, think about whether the author's words are positive or negative. A word such as *enterprise* has a positive connotation. Whereas the word *dull* has a negative connotation. To make an inference, use evidence from the text and your own knowledge of the topic to come to a new understanding of the text.

The intended audience for the argumentative article is _____

Write The author shows how he or she feels about young entrepreneurs by _____

_____

_____

? **Why does the author use a graph to help you see how effective Better World Books has been at raising money?**

Talk About It Reread the section "For the Love of a Good Book." With your partner, talk about what you learned by looking at the graph.

Cite Text Evidence How does the graph help you understand how donating books can make a difference? Write text evidence.

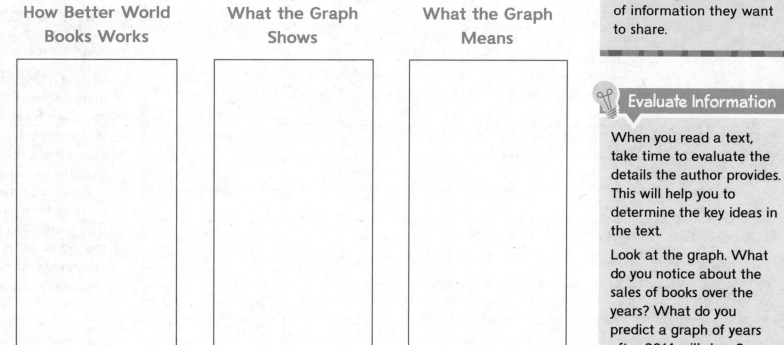

How Better World Books Works	What the Graph Shows	What the Graph Means

Write The author uses a graph to help me _____

_____

_____

_____

Respond to Reading

COLLABORATE

Discuss the prompt below. Apply your own knowledge of the author's point of view to inform your answer. Use your notes and graphic organizer.

How does the author make his or her point of view clear in this selection? Cite evidence from the text.

_____

_____

_____

_____

_____

_____

_____

_____

_____

_____

_____

_____

Starting a Successful Business

1   Becoming an entrepreneur is hard work. But if you're dedicated and have excellent organizational skills, it can be rewarding—sometimes, a small idea can become a very successful business! Neale S. Godfrey, author of *Ultimate Kids' Money Book*, shares these tips for a booming business.

2   **Step 1 Have an innovative idea.**

Suppose you like dogs, have free time, and feel compassionate toward people with busy schedules. Why not start a dog-walking service?

Literature Anthology:
pages 44–45

Reread and use the prompts to take notes in the text.

Underline words and phrases in paragraph 1 that tell what the author thinks about what it takes to become an entrepreneur. Write them here.

1 _____

2 _____

3 _____

COLLABORATE

Reread paragraph 2. Talk with a partner about how the author helps you understand what the word *innovative* means.

Circle clues in the illustration that support the text.

How do the illustrations help you understand the steps to starting a business?

Talk About It Reread the excerpt on page 73. Talk with a partner about the illustration and what it shows.

Cite Text Evidence What extra information do you get from the picture? Write clues in the chart.

Text Evidence	Picture Clues

Write The illustration helps me learn more about starting a business by _____

_____

_____

_____

Evaluate Information

Evaluating the photographs and illustrations in a text helps you better understand what you are reading. Ask yourself these questions.

• Why did the author include this image?

• What does the image help me understand about the topic?

Procedural Text

Readers to Writers

You can include procedural text in your own writing. If you want to explain a process or how to do something, consider numbering the different steps in the process. You can also make a chart of the different steps and add pictures to illustrate each step.

Procedural text explains how to do something in order or as steps in a process. Procedural texts often include

- instructions on how to do something
- labeled or numbered steps
- pictures or diagrams showing materials or how to perform a step

 FIND TEXT EVIDENCE

On page 45 in "Starting a Successful Business" the author uses procedural text to explain how to be a young entrepreneur. By numbering and describing each step of the process, the author explains the steps in a clear way.

Step 1 Have an innovative idea.

Step 2 Find out if your business has a chance of succeeding.

Step 3 Compile a business plan and a budget.

Step 4 Contact potential customers.

Step 5 Keep tabs on your business.

COLLABORATE
Your Turn Reread the steps you can take to start a business on page 45 of the **Literature Anthology**.

- What does the procedural text structure make you think about when

  starting a business? _____

_____

MAKE CONNECTIONS

Text Connections

? **What message do the authors of the "Helping Others Is Good Business" Blast, "Miller Boy," "Kids in Business," and "Starting a Successful Business" want you to know about running a business?**

Talk About It With a partner, read the traditional folk song "Miller Boy." A miller was someone who ground grain into flour and sold it. Talk with a partner about how the song tells what the miller boy does to earn money.

Cite Text Evidence **Circle** clues in the song that help you understand how the miller boy runs his business.

Write The author of the song and this week's selections want you to know that _____

_____

_____

_____

_____

_____

_____

_____

Quick Tip

There are many positive words in the song (*happy, goodwill, wealth*). These positive words help readers understand the songwriter's positive message about the miller boy and his business. Readers can compare this message to messages in other texts they have read.

Miller Boy

Oh happy is the miller boy who lives
by the mill,
He takes his toll with a free goodwill;
One hand in the hopper and the other
in the sack,
The ladies step forward and the gents
step back.

Oh happy is the miller boy who lives
by himself,
As the wheel goes 'round,
He gathers in his wealth;
One hand in the hopper and the other
in the sack,
As the wheel goes around the boys
fall back.

Phrasing and Rate

How we read text affects how well we understand the material. Commas, quotation marks, and other punctuation marks indicate **phrasing**, or the way ideas are grouped together. **Rate,** on the other hand, is how fast or slowly a person reads. When readers find the information easy to read, sometimes they read faster. Paying attention to phrasing and rate can make a text easier to understand.

Quick Tip

Writers sometimes use commas and a direct quotation to point out important information or places where the reader might want to read more slowly.

Page 60

Mycoskie is pleased and surprised. "I always thought I would spend the first half of my life making money and the second half giving it away," Mycoskie says. "I never thought I could do both at the same time."

Quotation marks indicate dialogue, or someone speaking. Readers might want to adjust their rate and slow down, pausing as a real speaker might pause, to achieve the correct phrasing.

Your Turn Turn back to pages 59 and 60. Take turns reading the section "Hearts and Soles" aloud with a partner. Pay attention to the phrasing and rate of your reading. How does the writer help the reader know when important information is coming? How does the writer help the reader slow down?

Afterward, think about how you did. Complete these sentences.

I remembered to _____

Next time I will _____

Expert Model

Literature Anthology:
pages 40–43

Features of an Opinion Essay

An opinion essay is a form of argumentative text. The author presents an opinion or claim about a topic and tries to persuade the audience to come to the same conclusion. Persuasive or argumentative writing

- clearly states the writer's opinion about a topic

- provides reasons and evidence to support that opinion

- provides a strong conclusion

Word Wise

The author uses social studies content words such as *patents, foundation, businesses* (page 41), and *product, manager, charity* (page 42) to show how these kids are real business people.

Analyze an Expert Model Studying argumentative text will help you learn how to write an opinion essay. **Reread** page 41 of "Kids in Business" in the **Literature Anthology**. Write your answers below.

How does the author of "Kids in Business" feel about young entrepreneurs? _____

What evidence does the author give to support that opinion? _____

_____

_____

Identify the audience for this article and explain your answer.

_____

_____

_____

Plan: Choose Your Topic

Brainstorm With a partner or a small group, talk about how much recess time you have at school. Discuss why you think you should have more (or less) recess time. List some of your reasons below.

_____

_____

_____

Writing Prompt Write an opinion essay about the amount of recess time you think students should be allowed to have during the week.

My opinion is that kids should have _____

_____

Purpose and Audience An **author's purpose** is his or her main reason for writing. Look at the three purposes for writing below. Underline your purpose for writing a persuasive article.

to inform, or teach   to persuade, or convince   to entertain

Think about the audience for your essay. Will your audience be teachers or a principal? What kinds of evidence—facts and examples—would persuade them that recess is good (or bad) for students?

Plan In your writer's notebook, make a Reasons and Evidence Chart to plan your writing. Use the list you made above to help you fill in the reasons and evidence for your opinion.

Quick Tip

To help you identify the reasons and evidence you will use in your writing, ask yourself these questions.

- *What reasons do I have for my opinion?*

- *What facts can I use to support my reasons?*

- *What examples can I use to support my reasons?*

Reasons	Evidence

Plan: Strong Opening

State Your Opinion A strong introduction gets the reader's attention by clearly stating an opinion, or claim, about a topic. Read the introduction below from "Kids in Business" on page 41 in the **Literature Anthology**.

> Starting a business is a huge undertaking. That's why these young entrepreneurs who help others are nothing short of amazing.

The use of adjectives such as *huge* and *amazing* emphasizes the writer's feelings about the topic. Use the opinion statement above as a model to write an introduction for your essay.

_____

_____

_____

_____

Research Pros and Cons Use digital or print resources to research facts about the advantages and disadvantages of recess time. Keep track of your reasons and evidence by writing your notes in your chart.

Digital Tools
For more information on writing an opinion, watch the "Opinion Statement" tutorial. Go to **my.mheducation.com**.

Draft

Reasons and Evidence Writers support their opinion with reasons, facts, and evidence. The author of "Dollars and Sense," on pages 58–61, argues that companies can help others and still make money. Read the paragraph below from "Dollars and Sense."

> One way the company raises funds for charity is by selling a line of T-shirts. The process starts with rock stars designing the art that goes on the shirts. Then the shirts are sold on the Internet. Part of the money that is raised from the sales of the shirts is given to charity.

Draw a box around the sentence that states the main idea of the paragraph. Then **underline** the evidence that supports the main idea. How does the paragraph provide evidence that supports the author's opinion that companies can make money while helping others? Write your answer below.

_____

_____

_____

Write a Draft Use your Reasons and Evidence Chart to help you write your draft in your writer's notebook. Think about what kind of facts and examples you want to include in your essay to support your opinion.

Revise

Transitions Writers use transition words and phrases to connect ideas. Words and phrases such as *however, also, although, therefore* and *as a result* show the relationship between ideas in an opinion essay. Read the paragraph below. Add transition words or phrases to connect the ideas.

> I think that I should be able to have a cell phone. I am starting fifth grade next fall. I will be walking to school. It is a 20-minute walk to school. I will need to call you if there is an emergency. Cell phones are expensive. You can give me your old cell phone.

_____

_____

_____

_____

Revision As you revise your draft, reread your introduction to make sure your opinion is clearly stated. Confirm that you also have enough relevant facts and examples to support your opinion. Include at least one counterclaim—a claim that could be made by someone who disagrees with your opinion—that you dismiss with evidence. Use transitions to connect your ideas.

Peer Conferences

Review a Draft Listen actively as your partner reads his or her work aloud. Take notes about what you liked and what was difficult to follow. Begin by telling what you liked about the draft. Ask questions to clarify information. Make suggestions you think will make the writing stronger. Use these sentence starters.

I like your introduction because . . .

I think you need more facts to support . . .

I wonder if you could add a better transition . . .

Partner Feedback After your partner gives you feedback on your draft, write one of the suggestions that you will use in your revision. Refer to the rubric on page 85 as you give feedback.

Based on my partner's feedback, I will _____

_____

_____

After you finish giving each other feedback, reflect on the peer conference. What was helpful? What might you do differently next time?

Revision As you revise your draft, use the Revising Checklist to help you figure out what text you may need to move, elaborate on, or delete. Remember to use the rubric on page 85 to help with your revision.

Revising Checklist

- [ ] Does my writing have a strong introduction?
- [ ] Did I include enough facts and examples to support my reasons?
- [ ] Did I use good transitions to show the connections between ideas?
- [ ] Do I have a strong conclusion?

Edit and Proofread

When you **edit** and **proofread** your writing, you look for and correct mistakes in spelling, punctuation, capitalization, and grammar. Reading through a revised draft multiple times can help you make sure you're catching any errors. Use the checklist below to edit your sentences.

✓ Editing Checklist

- ☐ Do all sentences begin with a capital letter and end with a punctuation mark?
- ☐ Is there noun and verb agreement?
- ☐ Do commas and linking words connect dependent clauses?
- ☐ Are possessive nouns and contractions used correctly?
- ☐ Are proper nouns capitalized?
- ☐ Are words with suffixes spelled correctly?

List two mistakes you found as you proofread your essay.

1 _____

_____

2 _____

_____

Quick Tip

When proofreading, don't try to read the essay for meaning. Instead, focus on one sentence at a time, and double-check spelling, punctuation, and grammar. Move your pencil from word to word as you read to check for errors.

Grammar Connections

Remember that a suffix sometimes changes the spelling of a base word: *happy/happily, create/ creative, begin/beginner, human/humanity.* For some words, you might have to change *y* to *i*, drop the silent *e*, or double a final consonant. Use a dictionary to be sure the word's spelling is correct.

Publish, Present, and Evaluate

Publishing When you **publish** your writing, you create a clean, neat final copy that is free of mistakes. Write legibly in cursive or type your work on the computer. Adding visuals can make your writing more interesting. Consider including illustrations, photos, or charts/graphs.

Presentation When you are ready to **present** your work, rehearse your presentation. Use the Presenting Checklist to help you. As you express your opinion, remember to speak loud enough, using appropriate volume.

Evaluate After you publish your writing, use the rubric below to **evaluate** your writing.

What did you do successfully? _____

What needs more work? _____

_____

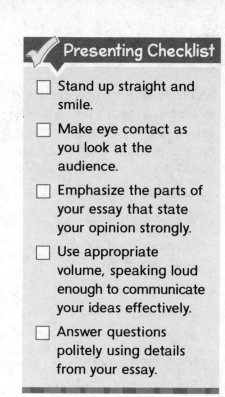

✓ Presenting Checklist

- ☐ Stand up straight and smile.
- ☐ Make eye contact as you look at the audience.
- ☐ Emphasize the parts of your essay that state your opinion strongly.
- ☐ Use appropriate volume, speaking loud enough to communicate your ideas effectively.
- ☐ Answer questions politely using details from your essay.

4	3	2	1
• gives a clear opinion supported by facts and other evidence • writing clearly shows that the writer's purpose is to persuade readers • has a strong introduction and a strong conclusion	• gives a clear opinion mostly supported by facts and other evidence • most of the writing shows that the writer's purpose is to persuade readers • has a satisfactory introduction and conclusion	• gives an opinion with limited facts and evidence • makes some effort to persuade readers • introduction and conclusion are missing key information	• gives an opinion but lacks facts and evidence • does not try to persuade readers • introduction is not strong and essay lacks a conclusion

Spiral Review

You have learned new skills and strategies in Unit 1 that will help you read more critically. Now it is time to practice what you have learned.

- Author's Purpose
- Compare-and-Contrast Text Structure
- Diagrams
- Dialogue
- Idioms
- Main Idea and Details
- Problem and Solution
- Suffixes

Connect to Content

- Create a Venn Diagram
- Make a Persuasive Poster
- Create a Fact Card

Read the selection and choose the best answer to each question.

Landforms Shaped by WEATHERING AND EROSION

1   In Palo Duro Canyon, Texas, bands of red, brown, and white show years of history. Hikers admire rock formations on treks. Visitors are amazed by the canyon's size and depth. People across the United States are overwhelmed by the extraordinary beauty of Palo Duro Canyon. But how did this canyon take shape? The answer is weathering and erosion.

Weathering

2   Weathering is the slow process of breaking down rocks into smaller pieces. Rain, wind, ice, and flowing water are some of the causes of weathering. Have you ever noticed the ragged sections of mountains? These ragged areas are caused by weathering.

Erosion

3   In contrast, erosion is the moving of rocks and soil by wind, water, gravity, or ice to another place. Gravity moves rocks downhill. Rain carries rock particles into rivers. Then the moving water carries the small pieces of rock and soil downhill. The particles in water can carve rocks into valleys. But it takes a very long time.

Zack Frank/Shutterstock.com

4   Wind and ice cause erosion, too. A lot of energy is needed to move rocks and soil particles by wind. Powerful winds can break down large rocks into smaller pieces. Then water can carry away those pieces. The type of rock and the intensity of the wind will affect the rate at which erosion occurs. For example, hard rocks take longer to erode than softer rocks. Yet no rock is safe from erosion. Like the wind, ice has the <u>ability</u> to erode landforms. Ice and large sheets of ice called *glaciers* move rocks from the ground. A glacier scratches, breaks, or carries away the things in its path.

Wind

Rain

Ice

WEATHERING
Wind, rain, and ice break up rock

EROSION
Moves broken rock and soil

"The Grand Canyon of Texas"

5   *Palo Duro* means "hard wood." It is the second largest canyon in the United States. Like other canyons, Palo Duro was shaped by erosion. The

Prairie Dog Town Fork of the Red River formed the lovely landscape and rock structures. The bands along the walls show four historical periods and span more than 240 million years. Palo Duro has become a wonder in the state of Texas because of weathering and erosion.

Palo Duro Canyon	Grand Canyon
120 miles long	277 miles long
20 miles wide (max)	18 miles wide (max)
800–1,000 feet deep	6,000 feet deep (max)

1 Reread paragraphs 2 and 3. Which text structure does the author use?

   A sequence

   B make inference

   C compare and contrast

   D problem and solution

2 The suffix *-ity* means "the quality of being." This information helps the reader know that the word <u>ability</u> in paragraph 4 means –

   F unable to do something

   G being in a good mood

   H not being useful

   J able to do something

3 Read the diagram on page 87. What causes rocks and soil to move?

   A weathering

   B rocks

   C erosion

   D lightning

> **Quick Tip**
>
> To find the main idea of a text, look for the most important point the author makes in the first paragraph.

4 Which of the following is the main idea of the text?

   F Erosion is the main cause of weathering.

   G Weathering and erosion can create canyons over time.

   H Weathering affects the climate where canyons are.

   J Erosion causes weathering in the Palo Duro Canyon.

Read the selection and choose the best answer to each question.

A Cinco de Mayo VISIT

1   "Wake up!" Leslie shook Vida, who was sound asleep. "C'mon! It's Cinco de Mayo!"

2   "Wha—? It's 6:00 in the morning!" Vida mumbled, rolling over and covering her head with the pillow.

3   "You know we get started early! We have *mole poblano, chalupas,* and *chiles en nogada* to prepare. Then we have to get ready for the parade! You brought your dress, right? Last year you forgot and—"

4   "*Sí,* I have the dress . . ." Vida responded sulkily, slowly realizing she wasn't going back to sleep.

5   Leslie's mom and Vida's mom were sisters. Vida and her family lived in Mexico, while Leslie's family lived in Houston, Texas. Every year, Vida was forced to visit her cousins. To make matters worse, she visited during Cinco de Mayo. Leslie thought May 5 was the best thing since sliced bread, but Vida wasn't so sure.

6   "Why do Americans celebrate Cinco de Mayo?" Vida asked. "It's not a big celebration in Mexico. Some of the banks don't even close."

7   "You know the story. In 1862, Mexican troops defeated French soldiers during the *Batalla de Puebla* in the Franco-Mexican War. The war was just beginning, but the battle showed their courage . . ."

8   ". . . and it became a symbol of patriotism and unity. That doesn't explain why you are waking me up at 6:00 a.m., though!"

9   Later, after the food was prepared, the girls changed into their dresses.

10   "Why do we have to wear this?" Vida complained.

11   "*Abuela* made them for us, and I have something new to add, too."

12   Leslie presented two beaded necklaces.

13   "I noticed some of the girls wearing them last year, so I made them for us!"

14   Vida held the special necklace in her hands. The colors of the Mexican flag alternated through the strand—green, white, red. She gently put it on and suddenly felt happy to have Leslie as a cousin.

15   As they looked in the mirror, Vida had to admit they looked great. Was Leslie's excitement starting to rub off on her?

16   "The clothing is definitely more colorful this year, don't you think? Oh, look!" Leslie exclaimed, pointing to some dancers in the parade.

17   Vida actually agreed—the parade was fantastic! Then a mariachi band marched past. She heard a *vihuela* playing a familiar tune. Vida had heard that song played on a guitar before, but for some reason, this was different. Vida's feet started moving, and her arms started swinging. Before she knew what was happening, she was dancing to the song, just like she did back in Mexico!

18   Leslie couldn't believe her eyes. "Vida what are you doing?!"

19   "I think I'm finally starting to understand why you love Cinco de Mayo so much! Let's dance!"

1   What does "best thing since sliced bread" in paragraph 5 mean?

   A   Something is amazing.

   B   The bread was sliced.

   C   Bread is amazing.

   D   Something fell apart.

2   The problem in the story is that –

   F   Leslie doesn't want her cousin to visit.

   G   Vida doesn't care about Cinco de Mayo celebrations.

   H   Vida's dress doesn't fit anymore.

   J   Leslie forgot the story behind Cinco de Mayo celebrations.

3   One of the author's purposes for writing this story was to –

   A   compare how Mexicans and Americans prepare their meals

   B   show how to make necklaces for Cinco de Mayo parades

   C   identify everything Leslie does with her cousin when she visits

   D   explain how some Mexican-Americans celebrate Cinco de Mayo

4   Which dialogue shows a resolution to the problem?

   F   "The clothing is more colorful this year, don't you think?"

   G   "I think I'm finally starting to understand why you love Cinco de Mayo so much!"

   H   "Abuela made them for us, and I have something new to add."

   J   "It's not a big celebration in Mexico. Some of the banks don't even close."

> **Quick Tip**
>
> If you are not sure what a question is asking, first make sure that you understand the meanings of all the words in the question. Use context clues to help you figure out any unfamiliar words.

PROBLEM AND SOLUTION

COLLABORATE

Plot is what happens in a story. It often includes a problem and solution. A plot has a conflict, rising action, a climax, falling action, and a resolution.

Conflict is the problem the character faces. **Rising action** is what happens as the problem builds. **Climax** is when the problem is confronted. It is the turning point of the story. **Falling action** is what happens right after the climax. **Resolution** is when the problem or conflict is solved.

Pick a story from Unit 1 or another familiar story. Analyze it to complete the chart.

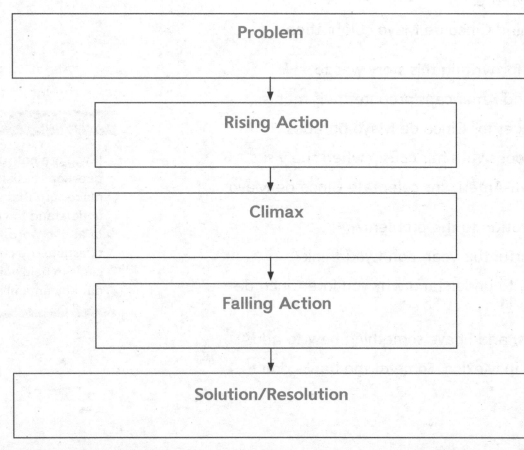

MULTIPLE-MEANING WORDS

Multiple-meaning words are spelled the same and pronounced the same, but have different meanings. *Feet* (fēt) can mean "the parts of a body" or "a measurement." **Homographs** are spelled the same but have different pronunciations and meanings. *Bow* (bō) is a tied ribbon. *Bow* (bou) is a gesture of leaning forward at the waist.

Use an online dictionary to define and hear the pronunciation of the words below. Fill in the information below.

desert

Definitions: _____

Multiple-meaning or homograph? _____

fair

Definitions: _____

Multiple-meaning or homograph? _____

SELF-SELECTED READING

Select a topic you are interested in learning more about. Choose a book about your topic for independent reading. After reading, decide what genre you will use to write your response. For example, you could write another chapter, a book report, or a letter in the voice of the main character. Compose your written response in your writer's notebook. Write the title of the book, the genre, and the topic below.

Title: _____

Genre: _____

Topic: _____

CREATE A VENN DIAGRAM

Venn diagrams show how two things are alike and different.

- Research two celebrations in your state. Create a Venn diagram to compare them. Use a variety of sources.

- Write facts and details about each celebration in a "Different" circle.

- Describe how the celebrations are similar in the "Alike" circle.

Different   Alike   Different

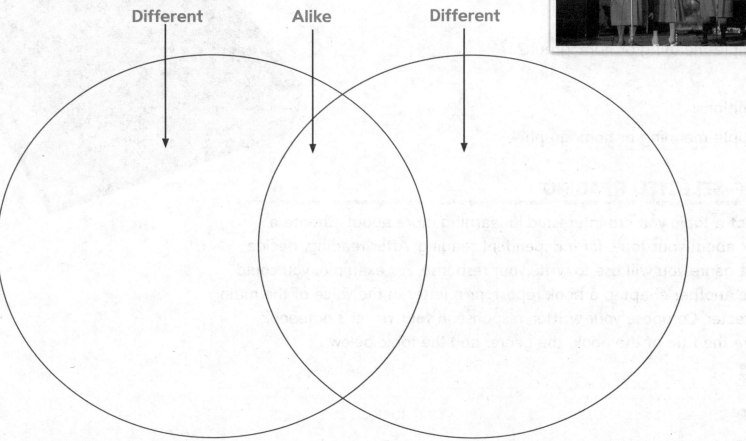

A.T. Willett/Alamy Stock Photo

MAKE A PERSUASIVE POSTER ABOUT SAND DUNES

The purpose of a **persuasive poster** is to convince people to take a specific action. For example, a poster about conserving energy might include a suggestion on how to use less electricity. Using facts to support your argument is an important part of convincing people to take action. Diagrams, charts, and illustrations are a good way to present facts.

Your poster on saving the sand dunes should include

- a diagram that shows how sand dunes erode
- a brief paragraph that explains how the erosion of sand dunes affects the ecosystem
- an action people can take to help save the sand dunes

Write ideas for your poster below.

_____

_____

My poster will convince readers by _____

CREATE A FACT CARD

A **fact card** shows images of the topic and provides interesting facts about the topic. You may wish to also include headings on your fact card.

- Research glaciers and the changes they made to Earth.
- Use your research to create an online or print fact card.
- Share your card with a partner or small group.

An interesting fact I learned about glaciers was _____

TRACK YOUR PROGRESS

WHAT DID YOU LEARN?

Use the rubric to evaluate yourself on the skills that you learned in this unit. Write your scores in the boxes below.

4	3	2	1
I can successfully identify all examples of this skill.	I can identify most examples of this skill.	I can identify a few examples of this skill.	I need to work on this skill more.

☐ Compare and Contrast ☐ Problem and Solution ☐ Main Idea and Details

☐ Multiple-Meaning Words ☐ Idioms ☐ Suffixes

Something that I need to work more on is _____ because

_____

_____

_____

Text to Self Think back over the texts that you have read in this unit. Choose one text and write a short paragraph explaining a personal connection that you have made to the text.

I made a personal connection to _____ because _____

_____

_____

_____

_____

Present Your Biographical Sketch

COLLABORATE

Discuss how you will present your biographical sketch. Use the presenting checklist as you practice your presentation. Discuss the sentence starters below and write your answers.

An interesting fact that I learned about the entrepreneur I chose is _____

_____

_____

I would like to know more about _____

_____

_____

Tetra Images/Getty Images

Talk About It

Essential Question

What helps an animal survive?

Look at the chameleon in the photograph. This little animal has adaptations that help it to survive in its environment. The chameleon can change its skin color to camouflage it from predators. It can wrap its long tail around branches.

Find other adaptations you think the chameleon has. Describe the chameleon's adaptations and tell how they help the animal to survive. Then talk with a partner about other animals and how they have adapted to survive.

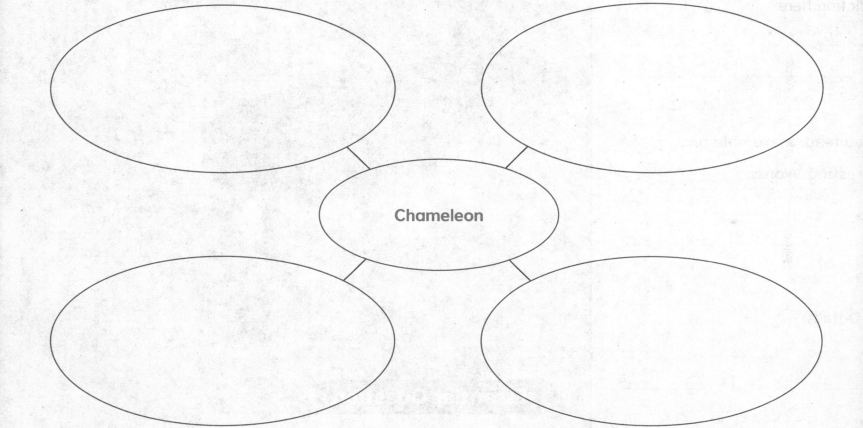

Chameleon

 Go online to **my.mheducation.com** and read the "Hidden in Plain Sight" Blast. How does camouflage help animals survive in their environment? Blast back your response.

TAKE NOTES

Preview the text by reading the title, headings, and captions and looking at the images. Then, predict what you will learn about from this selection. Write your prediction here.

_____

_____

_____

As you read, make note of:

Interesting Words _____

_____

_____

_____

Key Details _____

_____

_____

_____

_____

_____

_____

Animal Adaptations

Essential Question

What helps an animal survive?

Read about ways different animals adapt to their environments.

What would you do if you saw a skunk raise its tail? If you knew anything about skunks, you would run in the opposite direction! Skunks have a built-in survival system. They can blast a **predator** with a horrible-smelling spray produced by the glands under their tails.

The special ways that animals have to survive are called adaptations. These include physical traits such as the skunk's spray and animals with bright colors and markings that warn predators that they are **poisonous**. Some animals can sense the smallest **vibrations** in the ground. Others hear sounds from miles away. An adaptation can also be a behavioral trait. An example of a behavioral trait would be birds that migrate south every winter to avoid harsh temperatures.

When a skunk turns and sprays a predator, the foul-smelling mist can travel up to 10 feet.

Staying Warm

Brrrr! Imagine living in a place where the average annual temperature is an **extraordinary** 10° to 20°F. Welcome to the Arctic tundra of Alaska, Canada, Greenland, and Russia, home of the caribou. To stay warm, caribou have two layers of fur and a thick layer of fat. They also have compact bodies. Only 4 or 5 feet long, caribou can weigh over 500 pounds.

The tip of the caribou's nose and mouth is called a muzzle. It is covered in short hair. This hair helps to warm the air before they inhale it into their lungs. It also helps to keep them warm as they push snow aside to find food.

FIND TEXT EVIDENCE

Read
Paragraphs 1–2
Main Idea and Key Details
Circle the sentence that states the main idea in paragraph 2.

Underline the details about physical traits that help animals to survive.

Paragraphs 3–4
Summarize
Summarize the caribou's physical adaptations on these lines.

_____

_____

_____

_____

Reread

Author's Craft

How do the author's details about the caribou help you to make an inference about what animals need to survive in the Arctic tundra?

SHARED READ

FIND TEXT EVIDENCE

Read

Paragraph 1

Photograph and Caption

Underline the details in the text that support the photo and caption.

Prefixes

The prefix *un-* means "not." **Circle** the word that has the *un-* prefix. Write the word's meaning below.

_____

_____

Paragraph 2

Summarize

Write key details to summarize the adaptations of phasmids.

_____

_____

_____

Reread

Author's Craft

How does the author use the photo and caption to help you understand the phasmid's adaptation?

Finding Food

Every day, a caribou eats over six pounds of lichen! Caribou have unusual stomachs. The stomach's four chambers are designed to digest lichen. It is one of the few foods they can find in the winter. Even so, caribou still have a tough time in the coldest part of winter when their food sources decline. That's why they travel from the tundra to a large forest area, where food is easier to find. When the melting snow **dribbles** into streams, they know that it is time to return up north.

Lichen can grow in extreme temperatures.

Insects in Disguise

Look closely at the photo of the tree branch. Can you spot the insect? It is a phasmid. Some phasmids are known as leaf insects, or walking sticks. Phasmids look like leaves or twigs. These insects can change colors to really blend in with their surroundings. In this way, they are **camouflaged** from predators. It's as if they disappear from sight! These insects are nocturnal, which means that they are active at night. This is another adaptation that helps them avoid predators. It's hard to spot these insects in daylight, let alone at night.

This phasmid is called a walking stick because it looks like a stick with legs.

(bkgd) James H. Robinson/Oxford Scientific/Getty Images; (inset) Global Warming Images/Alamy Stock Photo

The alligator's physical adaptations include its log-shaped body. Other animals have trouble spotting the motionless alligator in the water.

Water, Please!

In Florida's vast Everglades ecosystem, the dry season is brutal for many plants and animals. Alligators have found a way to survive these dry conditions in the freshwater marshes. They use their feet and snouts to clear dirt from holes in the limestone bedrock. When the ground dries up, the alligators can drink from their water holes.

Other species benefit from these water holes, too. Plants grow there. Other animals find water to survive the dry season. However, the animals that visit alligator holes become easy **prey**. The normally motionless alligator may **pounce** on them without warning. But luckily, alligators eat only a few times each month. Many animals take their chances and revisit the alligator hole when they need water. In the end, it's all about survival!

Summarize

Use your notes to help you orally summarize the important information in "Animal Adaptations." Talk about whether your prediction on page 100 was confirmed.

EXPOSITORY TEXT

FIND TEXT EVIDENCE

Read

Headings

Why is "Water, Please!" a good heading for this section?

_____

_____

_____

Main Idea and Details

Underline all the details in the caption and text about adaptations that help an alligator to survive.

Make Inferences

What inference can you make about how the shape of an alligator helps it to survive?

Reread

Author's Craft

The author describes how alligators dig water holes to survive the dry season. How does that description show that one animal's adaptation helps and hurts other animals?

Vocabulary

Use the example sentences to talk with a partner about each word. Then answer the questions.

camouflaged

The green frog is **camouflaged** because it blends in with the grass.

What other animals are camouflaged in their environment?

_____

_____

_____

dribbles

Water **dribbles** down from the leaky roof.

What is something else that dribbles?

_____

_____

extraordinary

Schools were closed because of the **extraordinary** amount of snow in town!

What is an antonym for *extraordinary*?

_____

_____

poisonous

Some wild mushrooms are **poisonous** and can make you sick.

What other things are poisonous?

_____

_____

pounce

My cat loves to **pounce** on her toy mouse.

What other animals pounce?

_____

_____

Build Your Word List Pick one of the interesting words you noted on page 100 and look up its meaning in a print or digital dictionary. Pronounce the word and count the syllables. Write one statement and one question using the word. Share your two sentences with a partner.

predator

An owl is a **predator** that hunts for food at night.

What other animal is a predator?

_____

_____

prey

A mouse is **prey** for owls and other predators.

What do you think would be prey for a shark?

_____

_____

vibrations

When you strum on the strings of a guitar, you cause **vibrations** because the strings move back and forth quickly.

What else can make vibrations?

_____

_____

Prefixes

As you read, you may come across a word that you don't know. Look for word parts such as prefixes. A prefix is added to the beginning of a word and changes its meaning. Here are some common prefixes.

un- means "not"
re- means "again"
dis- means "opposite of"

FIND TEXT EVIDENCE

When I read the section "Staying Warm" on page 101 in "Animal Adaptations," I see the word extraordinary. *First, I look at the separate word parts. I know that* extra *is a prefix that changes the meaning of* ordinary. *The prefix* extra *means "beyond."*

Imagine living in a place where the average annual temperature is an **extraordinary** 10° to 20°F.

Your Turn Use prefixes and context clues to figure out the meanings of the following words.

disappear, *page 102* _____

revisit, *page 103* _____

Summarize

When you summarize, you retell the most important details in a paragraph or section of text. Summarize sections of "Animal Adaptations" to help you understand the information.

🔍 FIND TEXT EVIDENCE

Reread the section "Insects in Disguise" on page 102. Identify key details to summarize the section.

> Page 102
>
> **Insects in Disguise**
>
> Some phasmids are known as leaf insects, or walking sticks. Phasmids look like leaves or twigs. These insects can change colors to really blend in with their surroundings. In this way, they are **camouflaged** from predators. It's as if they disappear from sight! These insects are nocturnal, which means that they are active at night. This is another adaptation that helps them avoid predators. It's hard to spot these insects in daylight, let alone at night.

Phasmids are insects that can camouflage themselves to avoid predators. In addition, phasmids are nocturnal, which makes them difficult for predators to spot.

Your Turn Reread "Water, Please!" on page 103 and summarize the section.

_____

_____

_____

Photographs, Captions, and Headings

"Animal Adaptations" is an expository text. Expository texts give facts and information about a topic. They may include text features, such as **photographs, captions,** and **headings.** They can be organized with a certain text structure, such as compare-and-contrast or cause-and-effect.

FIND TEXT EVIDENCE

I can tell "Animal Adaptations" is an expository text because it gives me facts about how different animals have adapted. I see that each section has a heading. The text also includes photographs and captions.

Page 102

Finding Food

Every day, a caribou eats over six pounds of lichen! Caribou have unusual stomachs. The stomach's four chambers are designed to digest lichen. It is one of the few foods they can find in the winter. Even so, caribou still have a tough time in the coldest part of winter when their food sources decline. That's why they travel from the tundra to a large forest area, where food is easier to find. When the melting snow **dribbles** into streams, they know that it is time to return up north.

Lichen can grow in extreme temperatures.

Insects in Disguise

Look closely at the photo of the tree branch. Can you spot the insect? It is a phasmid. Some phasmids are known as leaf insects, or walking sticks. Phasmids look like leaves or twigs. These insects can change colors to really blend in with their surroundings. In this way, they are **camouflaged** from predators. It's as if they disappear from sight! These insects are nocturnal, which means that they are active at night. This is another adaptation that helps them avoid predators. It's hard to spot these insects in daylight, let alone at night.

This phasmid is called a walking stick because it looks like a stick with legs.

Photographs and Captions

Photographs illustrate what is in the text. Captions provide additional information.

Headings

Headings tell what a section of text is mostly about.

COLLABORATE

Your Turn Find and list two text features in "Animal Adaptations." Tell your partner what information you learned from each of these features.

_____

_____

Main Idea and Key Details

The main idea is the most important point that the author makes in a text or a section of the text. Key details give important information to support the main idea.

 FIND TEXT EVIDENCE

When I reread the section "Staying Warm" on page 101, I can identify the key details. Then I can think about what those details have in common. Now I can figure out the main idea of the section.

Main Idea
Caribou adaptations help the animal to survive the cold.
Detail
Caribou have two layers of fur.
Detail
Caribou have a thick layer of fat.
Detail
Short hair on their muzzles warms the air that they inhale.

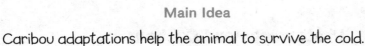

Your Turn Reread the section "Insects in Disguise" on page 102. Find the key details and list them in the graphic organizer on page 109. Use these details to figure out the main idea.

Quick Tip

An author may not tell you the main idea in the text. You may have to figure it out. Look for important details in the text, photographs, and captions. Use these sentence starters.

- *The details in the section is about . . .*

- *The photograph and caption are about . . .*

- *The main idea is . . .*

Main Idea
Detail
Detail
Detail

Respond to Reading

COLLABORATE

Discuss the prompt below. Think about how the author presents the information. Use your notes and graphic organizer.

How does the author use text features to explain animal adaptations and how they help animals survive?

_____

_____

_____

_____

_____

_____

_____

_____

_____

_____

_____

_____

Life-Cycle Diagrams

Life-cycle diagrams show the steps, or stages, a living thing goes through in its lifetime. A diagram usually includes photographs or drawings of each stage. Arrows point from one stage to the next. Labels or captions for each stage give information. Life-cycle diagrams help to make the information easy for the reader to see and follow. Here is how you should read a life-cycle diagram:

- Look closely at each part of the diagram.
- Follow the arrows that go from one stage to the next.
- Read the label and caption for each stage.

The life-cycle diagram on this page is about honeybees. What stage comes after larva?

Write it here. _____

 Make Life-Cycle Diagrams With a partner or in a group, research the life cycles of a cricket and a beetle. Use reliable sources to find the information. Then use the information to complete the following tasks.

- Make two life-cycle diagrams, one for a cricket and one for a beetle.
- Use labels and arrows to help readers follow the stages in a cycle.
- Write a paragraph to compare and contrast the two life cycles.
- After you finish, share your work with the class.

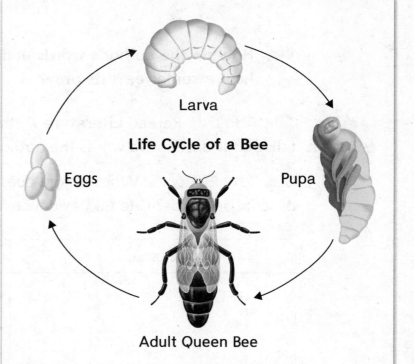

Larva

Life Cycle of a Bee

Eggs

Pupa

Adult Queen Bee

The diagram above shows the life cycle of a honeybee. What happens to the eggs? Write your answer here.

_____

_____

_____

_____

Spiders

How do the author's words and phrases help you visualize how a spider eats its prey?

Literature Anthology: pages 90–107

Talk About It Reread **Literature Anthology** page 94. With a partner, talk about descriptive words the author uses for how the spider eats.

Cite Text Evidence What image does the author create with these descriptive words? Cite text evidence from the paragraph.

Words	What I Visualize

Synthesize Information

Combine what you already know about adaptations. Think about the adaptations a spider has and how they help it to survive. Compare the way a spider gets and eats food with other animals you have learned about.

Write The author helps me visualize how a spider eats its prey by _____

_____

_____

? **How does the author help you understand how a spider uses its senses?**

Talk About It Reread page 98 of the **Literature Anthology**. Turn to your partner and talk about the way the author describes the body parts of a spider that sense things.

Cite Text Evidence What evidence does the author give that helps you understand his point of view about the spider? Write text evidence and explain the author's point of view.

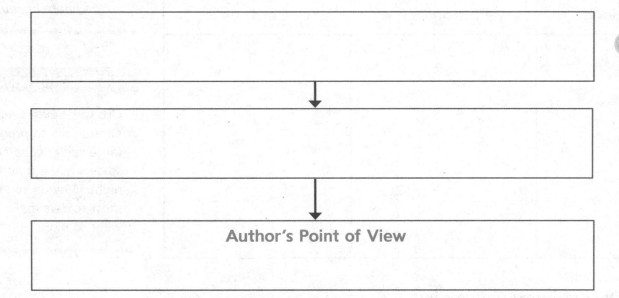

Author's Point of View

Write I know how the author feels about the spider's senses because

_____

_____

_____

Quick Tip

You can use these sentence starters when you talk about the author's point of view about the spider's senses.

- *The author thinks the spider's senses are . . .*

- *One of the reasons he feels this way is . . .*

Evaluate Information

Read all the details the author gives about spiders. When you review the information, you can evaluate if you agree with the author's point of view. How do you feel about spiders after reviewing all the details?

? **How do the text features help you understand more about orb web spiders?**

Talk About It Reread page 105 of the **Literature Anthology**. Look at the photograph and read the caption. Turn to your partner and talk about what new information you learned.

Cite Text Evidence What details in the text features give you more information about orb web spiders? Write text evidence in the chart.

Text Evidence	Photograph	Caption

Write The author uses text features to _____

_____

Respond to Reading

Discuss the prompt below. Use your own knowledge, your notes, and the graphic organizers to help you.

How do the text features help you understand the selection better?

_____

_____

_____

_____

_____

_____

_____

_____

_____

_____

Ingram Publishing/SuperStock

Quick Tip

Use these sentence starters to discuss the text and organize your text evidence.

- *The photographs help me understand . . .*
- *The captions explain . . .*
- *The text features help me . . .*

Self-Selected Reading

Choose a text and fill in your writer's notebook with the title, author, and genre. Record your purpose for reading. Include a personal response to the text in your writer's notebook.

Anansi and the Birds

Literature Anthology:
pages 108–109

1   Anansi always welcomed a challenge. His attempts to fool merchants out of their riches and lions from their jungle thrones made for exciting adventures. Today he would show those haughty birds that he could fly with the best of them.

2   He begged a feather from every bird he could find to create his own pair of wings, and then he began to practice flying. Anansi's wings camouflaged him well, and he looked just like a bird.

3   "Hoot!" the old owl chided under the moon. "A spider is not meant for the sky. Why do you try to be something you are not?"

4   "Mind your business, owl," Anansi replied angrily. "You are a predator, so go hunt some mice!"

5   Anansi followed the birds to their feast on top of a mountain peak. He helped himself to their fare, shoving birds aside to get his fill. When he was full, he fell into a deep sleep.

Reread paragraphs 1 and 2. **Circle** text evidence in paragraph 1 that tells you about Anansi's character.

COLLABORATE

Reread paragraphs 3 and 4. Talk with a partner about the relationship between Anansi and the old owl. **Underline** the dialogue that helps you understand how the owl feels about what Anansi is doing.

Then reread paragraph 5. How does the author hint that something unpleasant might happen to Anansi? **Draw a box** around the clue. Write it here:

_____

_____

6 Angrily, the birds took back the feathers from his wings and then left, all except for one crow. When Anansi awoke, he realized what had happened and begged the crow to help him get down the mountain.

7 "Of course," the crow replied slyly as he shoved Anansi over a cliff.

8 "Aaaayeeee!" shouted Anansi. Unable to fly, he tumbled helplessly through the air.

9 The old owl appeared before him, asking, "Why didn't you listen, Anansi? You are not a bird!"

10 "Please help me, owl!" pleaded Anansi.

11 The owl urged Anansi, "Push in your belly!" When he did, threads of silk shot out behind him. The owl caught them and tied them to a high branch. Dangling by threads, Anansi realized the owl was right. From that day on, he stuck to spinning webs instead of trying to be something he was not.

Read paragraphs 6–9. **Circle** the words and phrases that describe how the birds feel about Anansi, and what they did.

COLLABORATE

With a partner, read paragraphs 10 and 11. Talk about how the owl helps Anansi. **Number** the steps in the margin.

Then **underline** the sentence that tells how the spider feels about the owl now. Write the text evidence here:

_____

? **How does the author help you visualize the characters' traits so that you understand the lesson Anansi learns?**

COLLABORATE

Talk About It Reread the excerpt on page 116. Talk about each character's traits. How do the traits help you understand what each character is like?

Cite Text Evidence What details help you identify each character's traits? Record text evidence.

Reread the excerpt on page 116.

Anansi	Owl	Birds

What I Visualize

Make Inferences

What the characters say and do gives the reader clues about how a character may act in the future. This is making an inference. What do you think the relationship between Anansi and the birds will be like in the future?

Write The author helps me visualize the characters' traits to

help me _____

_____

_____

jaroon/iStock/Getty Images

Character

What a character says and does will tell the reader how the character thinks and feels. Sometimes, the way a character acts in the beginning of a story will change by the end. Those changes will help you understand the meaning of the story.

FIND TEXT EVIDENCE

In paragraphs 3–5 on page 116, the author describes how Anansi treats others. What word would you use to describe Anansi's character in this

section? _____

> "Hoot!" the old owl chided under the moon. "A spider is not meant for the sky. Why do you try to be something you are not?"
>
> "Mind your business, owl," Anansi replied angrily. "You are a predator, so go hunt some mice!"
>
> Anansi followed the birds to their feast on top of a mountain peak. He helped himself to their fare, shoving birds aside to get his fill.

Your Turn Reread the last two paragraphs on page 117.

- How does Anansi change from the beginning of the story to the end?

_____

_____

_____

On page 116, the author uses several homophones. Notice that the words *do* and *dew*, *peak* and *peek*, and *fare* and *fair* have the same pronunciation but different spellings and meanings. If you are not sure which word to use, look up a homophone's spelling or meaning in a dictionary. Find another homophone in the excerpt and use it in a sentence.

Readers to Writers

When you write, help your readers understand your characters. Describe how they look, speak, and interact with others. Use words that help your readers figure out the characters' personalities. For example, the author of "Anansi and the Birds" uses words such as *angrily* and *shoving* to describe Anansi's behavior. This description helps readers visualize the character.

Word Wise

On page 116, the author uses several homophones. Notice that the words *do* and *dew*, *peak* and *peek*, and *fare* and *fair* have the same pronunciation but different spellings and meanings. If you are not sure which word to use, look up a homophone's spelling or meaning in a dictionary. Find another homophone in the excerpt and use it in a sentence.

Text Connections

Think about the Blast and the selections you read in this unit. What have you learned about the adaptations that help animals to survive?

Talk About It Use the photograph and caption to talk about the leafy dragon seahorse. Discuss how the photograph shows how the seahorse survives.

Cite Text Evidence With a pencil, **trace around** the outside of the leafy dragon seahorse in the photograph. Reread the caption and **underline** what helps the animal protect itself from its predators.

Write The selections I read and this photograph show how animals are unique by _____

_____

_____

_____

_____

_____

_____

Leafy dragon seahorses, or leafy seadragons, live in the waters off the southern coast of Australia. They swim among the boulders and sea grasses in the reefs. These animals blend in with their environment to keep safe.

Kris Wiktor/Alamy Stock Photo

COLLABORATE

Present Your Work

Discuss how you will present your diagrams and paragraph to the class. You may want to plan a slide presentation or display the diagrams on the wall. Use the Presenting Checklist as you rehearse your presentation.

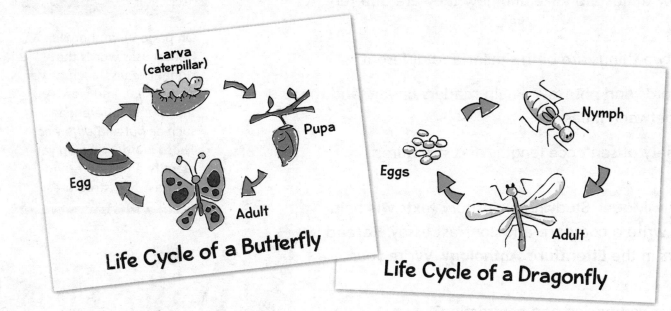

Life Cycle of a Butterfly

Larva (caterpillar)
Pupa
Egg
Adult

Life Cycle of a Dragonfly

Nymph
Eggs
Adult

Discuss the sentence starters below and write your answers.

The most interesting thing I learned about beetles and crickets is _____

_____

_____

I would like to know more about _____

_____

*Literature Anthology:
pages 90–105*

Expert Model

Features of a Compare-and-Contrast Essay

A compare-and-contrast essay is a form of expository text. It informs readers about how things are alike and how they are different. A comparison essay

- explains how two things are both similar and different

- uses linking words and phrases to help readers understand the relationships between ideas

- includes a variety of sentence lengths and structures

Word Wise

On page 91, author Nic Bishop uses words that signal likeness, such as *yet* and *similar,* and words that signal differences, such as *but* and *difference.* These words will help you identify a compare-and-contrast text structure.

Analyze an Expert Model Studying expository texts will help you learn how to write a compare-and-contrast essay. **Reread** page 91 of *Spiders* in the **Literature Anthology**. Write your answers below.

What is the author comparing and contrasting? _____

_____

How does the author vary the sentences? _____

_____

_____

_____

Studiohio/McGraw-Hill Education

Plan: Choose Your Topic

Brainstorm With a partner, make a list of animals and their adaptations, which help them to survive. Discuss how an animal's body structure or behavior helps the animal to move quickly or fly. Think about what helps animals survive in an extreme environment such as the desert or the Arctic tundra.

Writing Prompt Choose two animals from your list. Write a compare-and-contrast essay about the adaptations that help the animals survive in their environment.

I will compare and contrast _____

_____

Purpose and Audience An **author's purpose** is to inform, persuade, or entertain. The audience is the people who will read your essay. Write your purpose and audience below.

Purpose: _____

Audience: _____

Plan In your writer's notebook, make a Venn diagram to plan your writing. Label the middle circle with the name of both animals. Then label the name of one animal in the left circle and the name of the other animal in the right circle.

Grammar Connections

When using adjectives to compare two or more things, pay attention to the spelling of their comparative form (*taller, bigger, heavier*) and superlative form (*tallest, biggest, heaviest*). A wildcat is a large animal. Leopards are larger than wildcats. That tiger is the largest cat in the zoo.

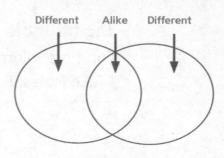

Different   Alike   Different

Plan: Compare-and-Contrast Text Structure

How are animal adaptations alike and different? There are similarities and differences among many animals. When you **compare,** you are describing how the animals are alike. When you **contrast,** you are describing how the animals are different. As you research and plan your compare-and-contrast essay about animal adaptations, answer these questions.

- What body structures are similar and different in the two animals?

- How are the animals' environments similar and different?

- How do the animals' adaptations protect them?

Now, write two more research questions about your animals.

1_____

2_____

Take Notes As you take notes on your topic, paraphrase information by putting it into your own words. Use your Venn diagram to map the similarities and differences between the two animals.

┌─ **Digital Tools** ─────────────────────────────
│
│ For more information on how to take notes, watch the
│ "Take Notes: Print" tutorial. Go to **my.mheducation.com**.
└──

Draft

Linking Words In a compare-and-contrast text structure, writers use linking words to help connect ideas. To show similarities between two things, writers may use linking words, such as *like, both, similar,* and *also.* To show differences between two things, writers may use linking words, such as *unlike, different,* and *but.* Read the text below and underline the words that show a comparison.

> The stomach of a caribou is similar to the stomach of a cow. Both use their stomach to digest food. The caribou's stomach has four chambers that help it to digest lichen. The cow's stomach is also divided into four chambers. This helps the cow to digest the grass it eats.

Now write a sentence that compares or contrasts two things about the animals you chose. Use a linking word to show a similarity or a difference.

_____

_____

Write a Draft Use your Venn diagram to help you with text structure as you write your draft in your writer's notebook. Don't forget to use linking words to help connect your ideas.

Grammar Connections

When writing about an animal in general, use the pronoun *it,* not *him* or *her.* And remember, a possessive pronoun does not have an apostrophe because no letters are missing. So *its long tail* is correct; *it's long tail* is not.

Quick Tip

As you draft your essay, remember that adjectives can help you convey information about your topic more clearly. Instead of just saying that one animal is larger than another, for example, you might also tell the size of both animals. Specific details will help your reader better understand how the two animals are alike and different.

Revise

Sentence Fluency The term *sentence fluency* means "how words sound together within a sentence, and how sentences sound when read one after the other." Use different sentence beginnings, transition words, and simple and compound sentences to make your sentences more interesting. Read the paragraph below. Notice the relevant details. Revise the paragraph so the text flows smoothly as you read it aloud.

> Polar bears have sharp claws. Brown bears have sharp claws, too. The claws help to protect the bears. A polar bear's white fur is an adaptation that helps it hide in a snowy environment. A brown bear's brown fur is an adaptation that helps it hide among trees in a forest.

_____

_____

_____

_____

Revision Revise your draft. Check that you present comparisons with good transitions. Read the draft to make sure you include relevant details, a variety of sentences, and no sentence fragments.

Grammar Connections

A simple sentence, or independent clause, shows a complete thought. A compound sentence has two independent clauses that are usually connected with a coordinating conjunction. Make sure your simple and compound sentences have a subject and a verb to avoid any sentence fragments. Also, the subject and verb in the sentence must agree.

Peer Conferences

Review a Draft Listen carefully as a partner reads his or her work aloud. Take notes about what you liked and what was difficult to follow. Begin by telling what you liked about the draft. Ask questions that will help the writer think more about the writing. Make suggestions you think will make the writing stronger. Use these sentence starters.

I like the way you used different kinds of sentences because . . .

Some linking words you might want to use are . . .

I wonder if it would sound better if you started the sentence with . . .

I don't understand this comparison. Can you explain how . . . ?

Partner Feedback After your partner gives you feedback on your draft, write one of the suggestions that you will use in your revision. Refer to the rubric on page 129 as you give feedback.

Based on my partner's feedback, I will _____

_____

_____

After you finish giving each other feedback, reflect on the peer conference. What was helpful? What might you do differently next time?

Revision As you revise your draft, use the Revising Checklist to help you figure out what text you may need to move, elaborate on, or delete. Remember to use the rubric on page 129 to help with your revision.

✔ Revising Checklist

☐ Does my writing fit my purpose and audience?

☐ Did I use a compare-and-contrast text structure?

☐ What details can I add or subtract to make the comparisons clearer and more relevant?

☐ Did I vary my sentence structures so that my writing has sentence fluency?

Edit and Proofread

When you **edit** and **proofread** your writing, you look for and correct mistakes in spelling, punctuation, capitalization, and grammar. Reading through a revised draft multiple times can help you make sure you're catching any errors. Use the checklist below to edit your sentences.

✔ Editing Checklist

- ☐ Do all sentences begin with a capital letter and end with a punctuation mark?
- ☐ Does every sentence have a subject and verb?
- ☐ Do commas or linking words connect dependent clauses?
- ☐ Are possessive pronouns spelled correctly?
- ☐ Are singular and plural nouns spelled correctly?

List two mistakes you found as you proofread your essay.

1 _____

_____

2 _____

_____

Tech Tip

Spell checkers are useful tools in word-processing programs, but they may not recognize wrong words, such as *its* when you mean *it's*. A careful review of your writing will help you find more errors.

Grammar Connections

When you edit and proofread, check that you have correctly placed commas. If you have compound sentences, make sure a comma separates the two complete ideas: *Ezra plays the piano, and Irma plays the trombone.*

Publish, Present, and Evaluate

Publishing When you **publish** your writing, you create a clean, neat final copy that is free of mistakes. Write legibly in cursive to complete the assignment. Consider adding visuals, such as illustrations, photos, or maps, to make your writing more interesting.

Presentation When you are ready to **present** your work, rehearse your presentation. Use the Presenting Checklist to help you.

Evaluate After you publish your writing, use the rubric below to **evaluate** your writing.

What did you do successfully? _____

What needs more work? _____

_____

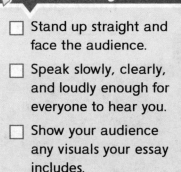

✔ **Presenting Checklist**

☐ Stand up straight and face the audience.

☐ Speak slowly, clearly, and loudly enough for everyone to hear you.

☐ Show your audience any visuals your essay includes.

☐ Point out the labels and details in the visuals.

☐ Answer questions politely using details from your essay.

4	3	2	1
• gives an informative, interesting, and detailed explanation of the topic • compares and contrasts information clearly, with strong transitions • includes different kinds of sentences	• informs readers with details about the topic • generally compares and contrasts ideas, but lacks some transitions • includes some different kinds of sentences	• attempts to tell about the topic but does not clearly explain it • some comparisons are difficult to understand due to lack of transitions • includes only a few different kinds of sentences	• does not focus on a particular topic • writing is disorganized, with no transitions between comparisons • includes no different kinds of sentences

Talk About It

Essential Question

How do animal characters change familiar stories?

COLLABORATE

The frog in the photograph is a handsome prince under a magic spell. That's how the familiar story goes, and of course it ends happily.

What are some of your favorite stories with animal characters? What are the characters' traits? Write some words that describe the traits of animals in stories. Talk about these traits with your partner. Remember to make eye contact as you speak. Enunciate and speak slowly and clearly.

Animal Character

BLAST BACK!
studysync

Go online to **my.mheducation.com** and read the "Cast of Animals" Blast. Think about animal characters you know from the stories you have read. Then blast back your response.

wildpixel/iStock/Getty Images

TAKE NOTES

To prepare to read, preview the play and make predictions based on the title and illustrations. Write your predictions here. Then, check your predictions as you read.

_____

_____

_____

As you read, make note of:

Interesting Words _____

_____

_____

Key Details _____

_____

_____

_____

_____

The Ant and the Grasshopper

Essential Question

How do animal characters change familiar stories?

Read about how an ant teaches a grasshopper an important lesson.

Scene I

(It is raining heavily on the African grasslands. Termite turns and sees the audience.)

TERMITE: *(Happily)* Yipes! I didn't see you. Welcome to the great plains of Africa! We're soggy now because it's the rainy season. Sorry. *(She shrugs and smiles.)* Today, we'll visit two very different friends of mine—Ant and Grasshopper. Maybe you have heard of them from other **familiar** stories. Let's see what my buddies are up to!

(An army of ants march in, carrying leaves filled with water. They approach Grasshopper, who lounges lazily under a plant.)

ANT: *(In a loud voice)* Company, halt! *(The ants stop.)*

GRASSHOPPER: *(Stretching and yawning)* Ant, old pal! Good to see you! I was just napping when I heard your feet pounding down the way. What's all the **commotion**?

SETTING
On the African grasslands
The present

CHARACTERS
Termite (narrator)
Ant
Grasshopper
An army of ants

Emily Carew Woodard

FIND TEXT EVIDENCE 🔍

Read
Termite Dialogue
Setting

Underline the sentence that tells you when this play is taking place. **Circle** the words that tell where the play is taking place. Why is knowing the setting important?

_____

_____

Stage Directions
Ask and Answer Questions

Draw a box around the text evidence that describes what the ants and the grasshopper are doing. What questions do you have about Grasshopper?

_____

_____

Reread
Author's Craft

Why might the author have chosen to make a play out of a fable?

SHARED READ

FIND TEXT EVIDENCE 🔍

Read

Ant Dialogue

Theme

Read all of Ant's dialogue. **Underline** the sentences that show Ant wants to teach a lesson to Grasshopper.

Ant Dialogue 4

Antonyms

Circle the antonym to the word *lazy* in the text. Based on what Ant has been saying to Grasshopper so far, which character do you think is wiser? Why?

_____

_____

Reread

Author's Craft

Compare the two scenes. What is the author's purpose for dividing the play into two scenes?

ANT: (*Looking* **annoyed**) Grasshopper, have you noticed what falls from the sky above you?

(*Ant stands at attention and points up at a cloud. Grasshopper sleepily rises and stands next to Ant. He looks at the sky.*)

ANT: Rain, Grasshopper! Rain falls from the sky! And when there is rain, there is work to be done.

GRASSHOPPER: (*Smiling then scratching his head*) Huh?

ANT: (*Sighing*) You should be collecting water for a time when it is unavailable. Instead, you lie here without a care for the future.

GRASSHOPPER: (*Laughing*) Oh, don't be so serious, ol' buddy! There is plenty of water now, and that's all that matters. You need to relax! You're much too tense. Why don't you make napping your new **specialty** instead of all this silly toil? Stop working so hard all the time!

ANT: (*Shaking his head as he grows* **frustrated**) The rainy season will not last forever, Grasshopper. Your carefree **attitude** will disappear with the water, and soon you will regret being lazy and wish you had been more energetic.

(*The ants march off as Grasshopper continues to laugh.*)

Scene II

(*It is a few months later, and the plains are now dusty, dry, and brown. Grasshopper, appearing weak and sickly, knocks on Ant's door. Ant, seeming strong and healthy, opens the door.*)

GRASSHOPPER: *(Nervously)* Hi there, pal . . . I was in the neighborhood. Boy, can you believe how hot it is? So . . . uh . . . I was wondering if maybe . . . by chance . . . you might have some water for your old friend.

(Ant tries to close the door, but Grasshopper quickly grabs it.)

GRASSHOPPER: *(Begging wildly)* PLEASE, Ant! I am so thirsty! There isn't a drop of water anywhere!

ANT: *(After a pause)* We ants worked hard to collect this water, but we cannot let you suffer. *(Giving Grasshopper a sip of water)* Do not think us **selfish**, but we can only share a few drops with you. I warned you that this time would come. If you had prepared, you would not be in this situation.

(Grasshopper walks slowly away. Termite watches him go.)

TERMITE: Although Ant has done a good deed, tired, **cranky** Grasshopper must still search for water. Grasshopper learned an important lesson today. Next time, he will follow Ant's advice!

Summarize

Review your notes and the predictions you made on page 132. Then, summarize what you read. Were your predictions correct?

FIND TEXT EVIDENCE

Read

Ant Dialogue

Theme

Underline the sentence that shows the lesson Ant was trying to teach Grasshopper.

Stage Directions

Read the entire page. **Circle** a stage direction that includes Ant and Grasshopper. How do you know which character speaks next?

_____

_____

Reread

Author's Craft

What is the author's purpose for including Termite in the play?

Fluency

Take turns reading the dialogue on page 134 with a partner. Talk about how the text features help you read the dialogue accurately.

Vocabulary

Use the example sentences to talk with a partner about each word. Then answer the questions.

annoyed

I was **annoyed** when my cats woke me up very early in the morning.

What is a synonym for *annoyed*?

_____

attitude

The girls had a good **attitude** when asked to volunteer for the book drive.

Describe your attitude about doing chores.

_____

_____

commotion

The ducks made a **commotion** with their quacking and splashing.

What is an example of something that can make a commotion?

_____

_____

cranky

Neil feels **cranky** when he is hungry.

What makes you feel cranky?

_____

familiar

I did not get lost because I took a **familiar** route from the bus stop to my house.

What is a familiar sound on the playground?

_____

Build Your Word List Reread the Termite's dialogue on page 133. Circle the word *soggy*. In your writer's notebook, use a word web to write antonyms for the word. For example, one antonym is *dry*. Use a thesaurus to look up other antonyms.

frustrated

The student was **frustrated** by the difficult assignment.

What makes you feel frustrated?

_____

_____

selfish

The two friends are not **selfish,** and they share everything.

How would you describe a selfish person?

_____

_____

specialty

My uncle is a good cook and his **specialty** is spaghetti.

If you were a cook, what would be your specialty?

_____

_____

Antonyms

As you read "The Ant and the Grasshopper," you may come across a word you don't know. Sometimes the author will use an **antonym**, a word or phrase that means the opposite of another word or phrase you might see in a nearby sentence.

🔍 FIND TEXT EVIDENCE

On page 134, I'm not sure what the word carefree _means. I can use the word_ serious _to help me figure out what_ carefree _means._

''Oh, don't be so serious, ol' buddy! There is plenty of water now, and that's all that matters. You need to relax!''

Your Turn Write an antonym for each word below in "The Ant and the Grasshopper." Write the meaning for each antonym.

halt, page 133 _____

tense, page 134 _____

sickly, page 134 _____

_____

Ask and Answer Questions

When you read a selection, you may not understand all of it. It helps to stop and ask yourself questions. As you read "The Ant and the Grasshopper," ask questions about what you don't understand. Then read to find the answers.

 FIND TEXT EVIDENCE

After reading Scene I, you may ask yourself what happens in Africa after the rainy season ends. Reread Scene II of "The Ant and the Grasshopper" to find the answer.

Page 134

> **Scene II**
> *(It is a few months later, and the plains are now dusty, dry, and brown. Grasshopper, appearing weak and sickly, knocks on Ant's door. Ant, seeming strong and healthy, opens the door.)*

I read that the land is <u>dusty, dry, and brown.</u> *Grasshopper is weak. This makes me understand that there are long periods of time when no rain falls in Africa.*

 Your Turn Why do authors use animals to tell stories? If you met the author, what questions would you ask about the characters in the play?

_____

_____

_____

Structure in Drama

The structure in a drama usually includes a list of characters, setting information, dialogue for the characters, scenes or acts, and stage directions. The scenes or acts divide the play into different parts.

FIND TEXT EVIDENCE

I can tell that "The Ant and the Grasshopper" is a drama. The author describes the setting. There is also dialogue, the lines that actors speak. The characters' names appear in capital letters before the lines they speak. The stage directions tell the actors what to do.

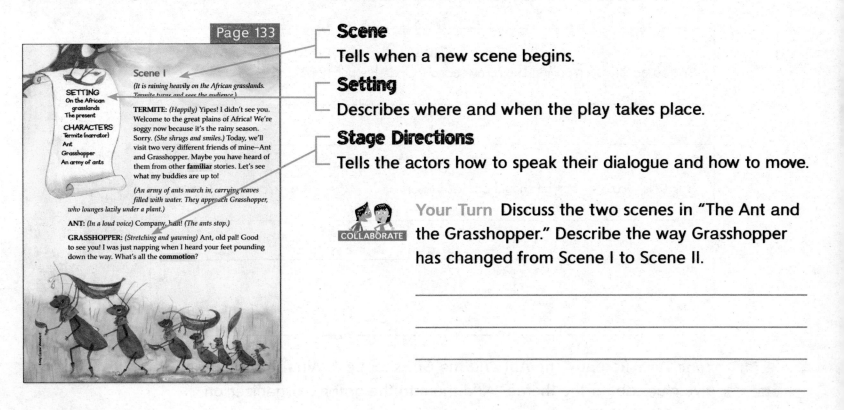

Page 133

Scene I

(It is raining heavily on the African grasslands. Termite turns and sees the audience.)

SETTING
On the African grasslands
The present

CHARACTERS
Termite (narrator)
Ant
Grasshopper
An army of ants

TERMITE: (*Happily*) Yipes! I didn't see you. Welcome to the great plains of Africa! We're soggy now because it's the rainy season. Sorry. (*She shrugs and smiles.*) Today, we'll visit two very different friends of mine—Ant and Grasshopper. Maybe you have heard of them from other **familiar** stories. Let's see what my buddies are up to!

(*An army of ants march in, carrying leaves filled with water. They approach Grasshopper, who lounges lazily under a plant.*)

ANT: (*In a loud voice*) Company, halt! (*The ants stop.*)

GRASSHOPPER: (*Stretching and yawning*) Ant, old pal! Good to see you! I was just napping when I heard your feet pounding down the way. What's all the **commotion**?

Scene
Tells when a new scene begins.

Setting
Describes where and when the play takes place.

Stage Directions
Tells the actors how to speak their dialogue and how to move.

Your Turn Discuss the two scenes in "The Ant and the Grasshopper." Describe the way Grasshopper has changed from Scene I to Scene II.

COLLABORATE

_____

_____

_____

_____

_____

Theme

The theme of a selection is the message, or lesson, that an author wants to communicate to the reader. To identify the theme, pay attention to the characters' words and actions.

🔍 FIND TEXT EVIDENCE

As I reread "The Ant and the Grasshopper," the different actions of Ant and Grasshopper in the rainy season seem like important clues to the theme. So do Ant's words about collecting water.

Look for details that help you figure out the theme.

Clue
Ant collects water during the rainy season. Grasshopper naps.

↓

Clue
Ant tells Grasshopper he should collect water.

↓

Theme

 Your Turn Reread "The Ant and the Grasshopper." What other details give clues about the theme? Add them to the graphic organizer on page 141. Use the clues to figure out the theme.

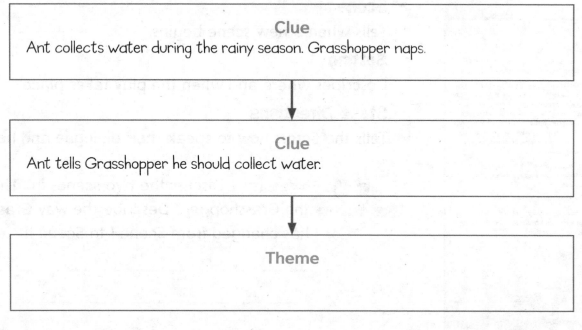

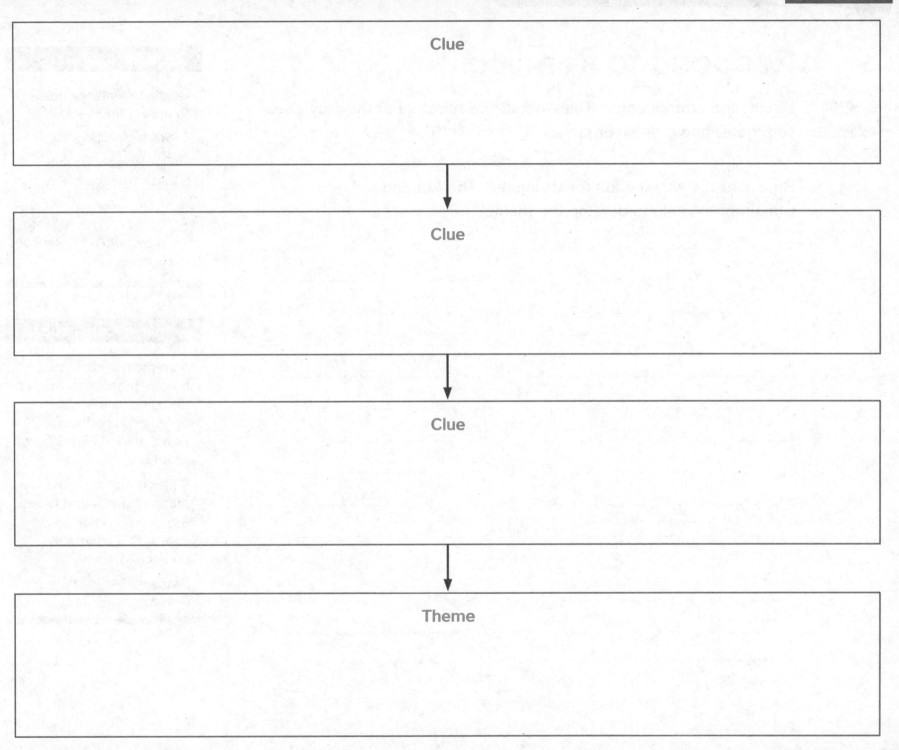

Respond to Reading

COLLABORATE

Discuss the prompt below. Think about the structure of the play. Use your notes and graphic organizer.

How does the way the author structures "The Ant and the Grasshopper" help to develop the theme?

_____

_____

_____

_____

_____

_____

_____

_____

_____

_____

_____

_____

_____

Food Web

A **food web** shows how plants and animals get energy, or food, in an ecosystem. A food web connects different food chains together. A food chain shows one path. For example, a food chain in the forest food web shows that a hawk eats a mouse and the mouse eats grass. The grass gets its energy from the sun. What kinds of plants and animals might you find in an ocean food web? Write your answer.

_____

_____

Forest Food Web

Make a Food Web Create a food web for a pond ecosystem. Research plants and animals that live in a pond and the food they eat. Start your food web with plants. Then, show the animals that eat those plants. Next, show the animals that eat those animals.

After you complete your food web, write a paragraph to predict what will happen if there are changes to the pond. For example, what happens if a pond becomes dry from a lack of rain? Think about the questions below.

• How does the change affect the food each living thing consumes?
• What happens if one of the living things disappears from the pond?

Use photos, illustrations, or digital graphics for your food web. After you finish, you will be sharing your work with the class.

The image above shows a forest food web. What living things are shown on this web? Write your answer below.

_____

_____

_____

ANCHOR TEXT

Ranita, The Frog Princess

Literature Anthology:
pages 110–125

? **How does the author help you understand what the Spanish words mean?**

Talk About It Reread the dialogue on page 114. Turn to your partner and talk about what helps you to understand the Spanish words in italics.

Cite Text Evidence What clues help you figure out each word's meaning? Record the words and clues here.

Word	Text Evidence

 Evaluate Information

The author tells you in the beginning of the play that the action takes place in Mexico. Review the characters' names and the Spanish words that appear throughout the play. How does the use of Spanish words and names in the play help give you a better sense of the setting?

Write I know what the Spanish words mean because the author _____

_____

_____

How do you know how the other characters feel about Felipe?

 Talk About It Reread **Literature Anthology** page 116. Turn to your partner and talk about how the author shows what the other characters in the play are feeling.

Cite Text Evidence Which words describe how the characters feel about Felipe? Use text evidence to explain how you know.

Character	⟶	Text Evidence
	⟶	
	⟶	
	⟶	
	⟶	

Write I know how the other characters feel about Felipe because the author _____

_____

_____

_____

? **How does the cultural setting influence the plot of the play?**

Talk About It Reread page 112. Turn to your partner and talk about where the characters are and what they are doing.

Cite Text Evidence What conclusion can you make about the society in which the characters live? Write the text evidence in the chart.

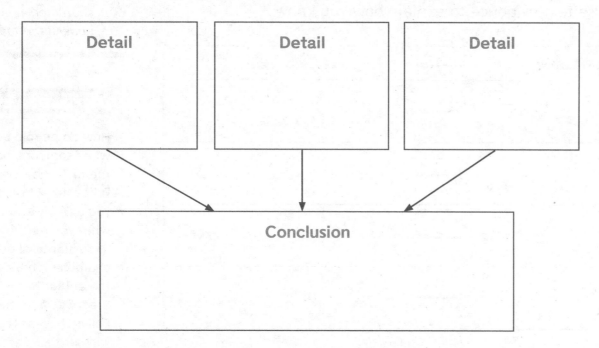

Detail	Detail	Detail

Conclusion

Write The author helps me understand the cultural setting by_____

_____

_____

_____

_____

Elnur/Shutterstock.com

Quick Tip

If you're having trouble keeping track of the characters in the play, go back and review the list of Players on page 111.

Make Inferences

Think about the things Man One, Man Two, and Man Three say to each other and the way Felipe responds to them. What inference can you make about the way life was in Mexico at the time the play takes place? How is Felipe's life different from the men's?

Respond to Reading

COLLABORATE

Discuss the prompt below. Apply your own knowledge about how people change, or don't change, over time. Use your notes and graphic organizer.

How does the author use descriptive language and stage directions to help you understand how the characters in the play change?

Self-Selected Reading

Choose a text. Read the first two pages. If five or more words are unfamiliar, pick another text. Fill in your writer's notebook with the title, author, genre, and your purpose for reading.

Pecos Bill and the Bear Lake Monster

*Literature Anthology
pages 128–131*

1   Have you ever heard of Pecos Bill? The cowboy raised by coyotes for seventeen years? The one who lassoed a tornado out of the sky using a live rattlesnake as a lariat? And dug the Rio Grande because his cattle felt thirsty and needed water?...

2   Pecos Bill was spending some time riding the range and herding cattle with a bunch of cowpokes. Late one night around a campfire, a cowpoke from Utah started telling stories about the Bear Lake monster. He said the monster looked like a snake with tiny legs and was over 100 miles long. One of the monster's favorite tricks was to suddenly appear in front of swimmers just to hear them shriek. Of course, it also ate a couple of those swimmers for lunch. Then there was the time a herd of pronghorn antelope went to drink from the lake. The snake slurped the whole herd down like it was nothing more than a big gulp of sweet tea. Another time, the monster had an itch on its tail. It got so frustrated trying to scratch that itch, the waves from the lake flooded the shore for days.

Reread paragraph 1. **Draw a box** around three things that show you Pecos Bill is a larger-than-life character. Write them here.

_____

_____

_____

_____

COLLABORATE

Discuss how the author uses descriptive language to describe the Bear Lake monster. What do the characters have in common?

_____

_____

_____

_____

_____

1 When Bill got to Bear Lake he was mighty hot and thirsty. He waded right into the cool, clear water and swam out a mile or two. All of a sudden, the water churned and foamed and ten-foot waves started crashing over Bill's head. A monster reared out of the water with its mouth open and roared. Bill had seen caverns smaller than that snake's mouth. Its roar shook the surrounding mountains. Without missing a beat, Pecos Bill jumped onto the monster's neck and slipped a loop of rope into its mouth. Then he held the ends like reins.

2 To say the snake was as cranky as a grizzly that's been stung by a swarm of hornets is understating the matter. The monster twisted and turned its scaly back trying to buck Bill off. But Bill didn't budge. The winds shrieked and howled around Bill, whipping up the waves to higher and higher peaks. So much water got splashed around that the whole lake turned into a giant waterspout!

Reread paragraph 2. **Circle** what happened to Pecos Bill when the monster tried to buck him off. **Underline** the descriptive language the author uses to help you picture what happens next.

Look at the illustration below and read the caption. Discuss how the snake changed from the beginning of the story to the end. Write the text evidence here.

_____

_____

The monster snake from Bear Lake, Utah, still lives in the loch to this day. Only now it's so shy and frightened that only a few people have ever seen it.

? **How does the author use the comparison of Pecos Bill to the Bear Lake monster to create suspense?**

Talk About It Reread both excerpts on pages 148–149. Talk with a partner about the descriptions of Pecos Bill and the Bear Lake monster.

Cite Text Evidence What clues does the author use to help build suspense? Write text evidence here and explain how it builds suspense.

Quick Tip

In the tall tale, there are anecdotes about Peco Bill's experiences with the monster. The anecdotes are short, amusing stories. They were written to entertain the reader. When you reread, look for the anecdotes.

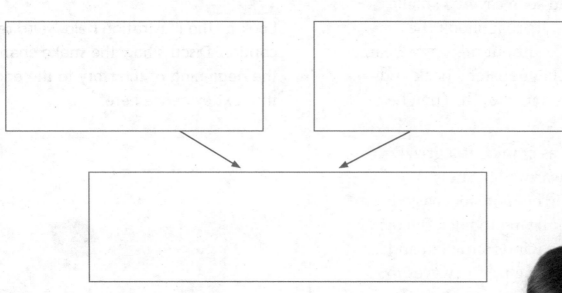

Write Why does the author use anecdotes, or background stories, to describe Pecos Bill and the Bear Lake monster?

_____

_____

_____

_____

Hyperbole

An exaggeration makes something sound bigger or better than it really is. For example, you are exaggerating if you say, "I'm so hungry I can eat a horse." Writers exaggerate to add drama to a story and make characters larger than life. Those exaggerations are called hyperbole. Exaggerations are often used in tall tales like the one you just read about Pecos Bill.

🔍 FIND TEXT EVIDENCE

In paragraph 2 on page 148 of "Pecos Bill and the Bear Lake Monster," the author uses hyperbole to tell what happens after the monster scratches an itch. The author tells us that the waves from the lake flooded the shore for days. We can tell that the author is exaggerating to make the monster an incredible, larger-than-life character.

> Another time, the monster had an itch on its tail. It got so frustrated trying to scratch that itch, the waves from the lake flooded the shore for days.

Your Turn Reread paragraph 2 on page 149.

• What words does the author use to describe what happened when Pecos Bill and the monster wrestled? _____

_____

• How does hyperbole help you picture the battle?

_____

Text Connections

? **How does Mary Howitt use words and phrases to help you visualize the characters in her poem? How is it similar to the way the authors describe the characters in *Ranita, The Frog Princess,* and "Pecos Bill and the Bear Lake Monster"?**

Talk About It Read the excerpt from "The Spider and the Fly." Talk with a partner about how the spider tricks and then traps the fly.

Cite Text Evidence **Circle** words and phrases in the poem that make the spider seem human. **Underline** text evidence that makes the fly seem human.

Write The selections I read and Mary Howitt's poem use words and phrases to help me visualize

_____

_____

_____

_____

_____

_____

_____

from
The Spider and the Fly

Alas, alas! how very soon this silly little Fly,

Hearing his wily, flattering words, came slowly flitting by;

With buzzing wings she hung aloft, then near and nearer drew, -

Thinking only of her brilliant eyes, and green and purple hue;

Thinking only of her crested head - poor foolish thing! At last,

Up jumped the cunning Spider, and fiercely held her fast.

He dragged her up his winding stair, into his dismal den.

—by Mary Howitt

Present Your Work

Discuss how you will present your food web to the class. Think about how it shows the ways living things are connected in a pond ecosystem. Use the Presenting Checklist as you practice your presentation. Discuss the sentence starters below and write your answers.

An interesting fact I learned about the living things in a pond is _____

_____

_____

I would like to know more about _____

_____

_____

Albaimages/Alamy Stock Photo

Essential Question

How are writers inspired
by animals?

COLLABORATE

Writers are observers. Their observations inspire them to create a picture of their experiences with words.

Look at the photograph. Identify dolphin and other animal traits that might inspire a writer. Then talk to a partner about a favorite animal and explain what kind of story, play, or poem you might write about it.

Animal Traits

BLAST BACK!
studysync

Go online to **my.mheducation.com** and read the "Inspiring Animals" Blast. Think about your favorite story about an animal. How are writers inspired by animals? Then blast back your response.

Rene Frederick/Photodisc/Getty Images

SHARED READ

ASK QUESTIONS

Asking questions helps you understand your purpose for reading. Preview the poems and write a question about one of the animals or poems.

_____

_____

_____

As you read, make note of:

Interesting Words _____

_____

_____

_____

Key Details _____

_____

_____

_____

_____

_____

_____

DOG

A brown boomerang,
my dog flies off, arcs his way
back into my arms.

— Jeffrey Boyle

Essential Question

How are writers inspired by animals?

Read how poets use creative thinking to write about animals.

THE EAGLE

He clasps the crag with crooked hands;
Close to the sun in lonely lands,
Ring'd with the azure world, he stands.

The wrinkled sea beneath him crawls;
He watches from his mountain walls,
And like a thunderbolt he falls.

— Alfred, Lord Tennyson

Emily Carew Woodard

FIND TEXT EVIDENCE 🔍

Read

Page 156
Point of View
Underline the word that helps you figure out the speaker of the poem. What is the speaker's relationship to the dog?

Page 156
Similes and Metaphors
Draw a box around the object that the poet compares his dog to.

Page 157
Meter and Rhyme
Circle the end rhymes in each stanza. Write the number of syllables in each line.

Reread
Author's Craft

What language hints at how the poet feels about the eagle? Use text evidence.

FIND TEXT EVIDENCE 🔍

Read

Page 158

Point of View

Underline the three pronouns in the first stanza. What point of view is the poem told from?

Lyric Poetry

Circle the rhymes in the first two stanzas. Read the second stanza aloud. Does the second stanza have a consistent rhythm or meter?

Reread

Author's Craft

How would the poem be different if the author had used a third-person point of view?

CHIMPANZEE

From branch to branch on outstretched arms,
From tree to ground I leap.
When I want to eat a snack,
I stick a stick in a termite heap.

I use my teeth to rip off leaves
And make the branch all bare,
Then find the hole the bugs come out
And patiently wait there.

My skinny branch becomes a bridge,
As brittle bugs climb up the stick.
I pick them off one by one
And crunch them like potato chips!

— Ellen Lee

Rat

Teeth like jackhammers,
I chew through concrete for fun,
bring the outdoors in!

— Rosa Sandoval

Make Connections

What animal would you write a poem about? What details about the animal would you focus on?

FIND TEXT EVIDENCE 🔍

Read

Page 159

Point of View

Underline the pronoun that shows the point of view of the speaker. Write the speaker of the poem on the line.

Similes and Metaphors

Circle the word that tells you the poet is using a simile. Write the two things being compared.

Haiku

How many syllables are in the first and last lines? Write the answer.

Reread

Author's Craft

Reread "Chimpanzee" and "Rat." Compare and contrast the two poems.

Vocabulary

Use the example sentences to talk with a partner about each word. Then answer the questions.

brittle

The dry, **brittle** leaf fell apart when I closed my hand around it.

What is something else that is brittle?

_____

_____

creative

Our team was **creative** and built robots for the competition.

Describe a time when you were creative.

_____

_____

descriptive

The zookeeper gave a **descriptive** talk about giraffes, telling what they look and act like.

Use descriptive language to discuss your favorite activity.

_____

_____

outstretched

Three seagulls glided through the air on **outstretched** wings.

What is an antonym for the word _outstretched_?

_____

_____

Poetry Terms

metaphor

"The huge garbage truck is a monster" is a **metaphor** because it compares two unlike things without using _like_ or _as_.

Give another example of a metaphor.

_____

_____

simile

"The long grass is like hair" is a **simile** because it compares two unlike things using _like_ or _as_.

Give another example of a simile.

_____

_____

rhyme

Two words **rhyme** when they sound the same, such as *claw* and *draw*.

What word rhymes with *fall*?

_____

_____

meter

Meter is the pattern of stressed and unstressed syllables in a poem.

How does a strong meter affect the rhythm of a poem?

_____

_____

> **Build Your Word List** Reread "The Eagle" on page 157. Underline two interesting words. In your writer's notebook, write the two words. Use an online or print thesaurus to find two synonyms for each word. Write the synonyms next to each word.

Similes and Metaphors

A **simile** is a comparison of two unlike things using the words *like* or *as*—for example, *straight as an arrow*.

A **metaphor** is a comparison of two unlike things without the words *like* or *as*—for example, *the grass was a green carpet*.

🔍 FIND TEXT EVIDENCE

When I read "Chimpanzee" on page 158, I see that the poet uses a simile in the last stanza to describe how the chimpanzee is eating the termites.

I pick them off one by one
And crunch them like potato chips!

Your Turn Reread the first stanza of "The Eagle" on page 157 and identify the metaphor. In your writer's notebook, rewrite the metaphor as a simile.

_____

_____

Alessandra Cimatoribus

Meter and Rhyme

Meter is the rhythm of syllables in a line of poetry. It is created by the arrangement of accented and unaccented syllables. (*Accented* means "stressed"; *unaccented* means "unstressed.") Words **rhyme** when their endings sound the same.

FIND TEXT EVIDENCE

Reread the poem "The Eagle" on page 157. Listen for the end rhymes and to the rhythm of the meter.

> He clasps the crag with crooked hands;
> Close to the sun in lonely lands,
> Ring'd with the azure world, he stands.
>
> The wrinkled sea beneath him crawls;
> He watches from his mountain walls,
> And like a thunderbolt he falls.

Rhyme *Say the last words of each line of the first stanza. They rhyme because their endings sound alike.*

Meter *Read the second stanza aloud. A stressed syllable follows each unstressed syllable, which makes the words "bounce."*

Quick Tip

To count the stressed and unstressed syllables in a poem, slowly read the words aloud. Exaggerate each stress and count each syllable on your fingers. To hear the rhymes in a poem, read the poem aloud. Pay special attention to the words at the end of each line.

Your Turn Find other words that rhyme in "The Eagle." Then identify whether the meter is the same in every line.

_____

_____

_____

_____

Lyric Poetry and Haiku

Lyric poetry

- expresses the thoughts and feelings of the poet
- often has end rhymes and a consistent, or regular, meter

Haiku

- uses three short lines to describe a scene or a moment
- has a first and last line of five syllables and a second line of seven syllables

 FIND TEXT EVIDENCE

"The Eagle" is a lyric poem because it tells how the poet feels about the eagle. It also has end rhymes and a consistent meter.

Page 157

THE EAGLE

He clasps the crag with crooked hands;
Close to the sun in lonely lands,
Ring'd with the azure world, he stands.

The wrinkled sea beneath him crawls;
He watches from his mountain walls,
And like a thunderbolt he falls.

— Alfred, Lord Tennyson

The poet describes the eagle as "close to the sun in lonely lands." I wonder if the poet feels the eagle is above other animals in other ways.

 Your Turn Reread the poem "Dog" on page 156. Identify the form of the poem and give evidence.

_____

_____

_____

_____

Readers to Writers

When you write a lyric poem, try including the same number of syllables in each line. Include rhymes at the end of every other line. This will give your poem a consistent meter. To help find words that rhyme, use a rhyming dictionary. Remember to include your thoughts and feelings about the topic of your poem.

Point of View

The voice you hear in a poem is the speaker. The speaker's point of view is how the speaker thinks or feels. Sometimes the speaker is a character in the poem. The speaker may be telling about the characters or events in the poem.

 FIND TEXT EVIDENCE

In "Chimpanzee," the pronouns I, me, *and* my *tell me that the speaker is the chimpanzee. I will reread the poem on page 158 and find the details that give me clues to the chimpanzee's point of view.*

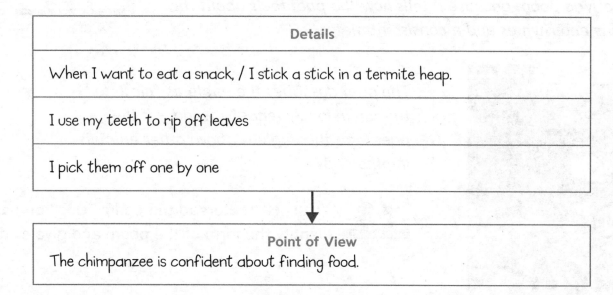

Details
When I want to eat a snack, / I stick a stick in a termite heap.
I use my teeth to rip off leaves
I pick them off one by one

Point of View

The chimpanzee is confident about finding food.

 Your Turn Reread "The Eagle" on page 157. Is the speaker a character in the poem? In the chart on page 165, list important details that give clues to the speaker's point of view. Then identify the point of view.

Quick Tip

Remember that you can use pronouns to identify the point of view of the poem. But point of view is also how the speaker thinks and feels about the topic of the poem. Use these sentence starters when speaking or writing about point of view.

- *The pronoun I tells me . . .*
- *The speaker feels . . .*

Details

↓

Point of View

Respond to Reading

COLLABORATE

Discuss the prompt below. Think about how the poets describe their animal and its actions. Use your notes and graphic organizer.

How do the poets use point of view and figurative language to portray animals?

_____

_____

_____

_____

_____

_____

_____

_____

_____

_____

_____

_____

_____

How to Create a Bibliography

A **bibliography** is a list of all the sources used for a research project. Bibliographies can include print, digital, and multimedia sources. Examples of sources that a bibliography might have are

- books
- magazines
- videos
- websites

What sources have you used for research projects?

_____

_____

Fun Animal Facts With a partner or a group, brainstorm animals that you want to learn more about. Choose an animal, then research five fun, unusual facts about it.

- Use the five facts to create a digital poster.
- Include photos and a video of your animal.
- Make a bibliography listing the sources you used.
- Share your poster and bibliography with the class.

BOOK

Author   Date of Publication   Title

Gemma, Vida. (2018). *The Best Dogs Around.* Cleveland: Paws Publishers.

Place of Publication   Publisher

WEBSITE

Author   Title of Page   Publisher

Johnson, Lija. *Whales Everywhere.* The Whale Society of American Animals, 2018. Web. 10 Aug. 2018.

Year   Medium   Access Date

Bibliographies include information about a source. In the list, the information is presented in a certain order, usually alphabetical.

Poetry

How does the poet use figurative language to help you visualize bats?

Literature Anthology: pages 132–137

Talk About It Reread "Bat" on page 133. Talk with a partner about what bats look like during the day and what they look like at dusk.

Cite Text Evidence What words and phrases help you picture the bats during the day and at night? Write text evidence in the chart.

Make Inferences

Identify the similes in the first stanza. Then identify the imagery in the second stanza. Use this information to make an inference about how the poet feels about bats.

Text Evidence	What I Visualize

Write The poet helps me visualize bats by _____

_____

_____

? **How does each poet use words and phrases to create a different mood?**

Talk About It With a partner, reread "The Grasshopper Springs" and "Fireflies at Dusk." Talk about how each poem makes you feel.

Cite Text Evidence What words help to create a certain mood in the poems? Write and explain text evidence in the chart.

Poem	Text Evidence	Why is this effective?
"The Grasshopper Springs"		
"Fireflies at Dusk"		

Write Each poet uses words and phrases to create a mood by _____

_____

_____

Respond to Reading

COLLABORATE

Discuss the prompt below. Apply your knowledge of being inspired by nature to write your answer. Use your notes and graphic organizer.

Describe how the poets use figurative language to show their point of view about each animal or insect.

_____

_____

_____

_____

_____

_____

_____

_____

_____

_____

_____

_____

_____

_____

_____

_____

Quick Tip

Use these sentence starters to talk about and cite evidence in the text.

- *In each poem, the poet uses figurative language to . . .*
- *In "The Sandpiper," the poet describes . . .*
- *In "The Grasshopper Springs" and "Fireflies at Dusk," the poets describe how . . .*

Self-Selected Reading

Choose a text and fill in your writer's notebook with the title, author, and genre of the selection. Include a personal response to the text.

Literature Anthology
pages 136-137

Fog

? How does the poet use words and phrases to help you visualize how fog is like a cat?

Talk About It Read "Fog" on page 136 of the **Literature Anthology** aloud to a partner. Talk about how the poet describes what fog is like.

Cite Text Evidence What words and phrases help you picture how fog is like a cat? Write text evidence in the chart.

Text Evidence	What I Visualize

Write The poet helps me visualize how fog is like a cat by _____

_____

_____

Quick Tip

When poets compare two unlike things, they are creating a simile or metaphor. This figurative language helps the reader visualize what the poet is describing. It also lends artistry to the poem.

White Cat Winter

? **How do the poets use words and phrases to create mood?**

Talk About It Reread the poems on pages 136 and 137 of the **Literature Anthology**. Talk with a partner about how each poem makes you feel.

Cite Text Evidence What words and phrases help create a mood in each poem? Write text evidence and describe the mood.

Text Evidence	Mood

Write The poets create mood by _____

_____

_____

Imagery and Assonance

Imagery is the use of specific language to create pictures and sounds in the reader's mind. To create imagery, poets use simile, metaphor, and sensory words and phrases. To create sound effects, the poet uses **assonance**, or the repetition of vowel sounds in the middle of words. Words with assonance can rhyme, like *cat* and *sat,* or just have the same vowel sound, like *row* and *bone.*

FIND TEXT EVIDENCE

In "White Cat Winter," on page 137 of the **Literature Anthology**, the poet uses assonance with the words *asleep, creeps,* and *beside.* They share the same vowel sound and two of the words also rhyme. By including assonance, the poet makes a connection between the ideas and creates a quiet mood.

Your Turn Read the poem "White Cat Winter" again.

• What other examples of assonance are in the poem? _____

_____

_____

• How does the assonance affect the ideas and mood of the poem?

_____

_____

_____

Text Connections

? **How does Lewis Carroll use the crocodile as inspiration for his poem? How is Carroll's poem similar to other animal poems you read this week?**

Talk About It Read "How Doth the Little Crocodile." Talk with a partner about how Lewis Carroll describes the crocodile.

Cite Text Evidence **Circle** words and phrases in the poem that help you visualize the crocodile.

Write The "Inspiring Animals" Blast, the selections I read, and this poem help me understand how poets and writers are inspired by animals. The way Lewis Carroll is inspired by the crocodile is like _____

_____

_____

_____

_____

_____

_____

_____

Quick Tip

Poets are inspired by the way animals behave, sound, look, smell, and other sensory details. By looking at the words the poet used, readers learn more about the poet's inspiration, such as a good or bad experience with an animal.

How Doth the Little Crocodile

How doth the little crocodile
Improve his shining tail,
And pour the waters of the Nile
On every golden scale!

How cheerfully he seems to grin,
How neatly spreads his claws,
And welcomes little fishes in
With gently smiling jaws!

— Lewis Carroll

Expression and Phrasing

Think about the meaning of a poem when you read aloud. Reading a poem with **expression**, or feeling, makes the poem more interesting and makes the ideas in the poem clearer. Commas, dashes, and other punctuation marks indicate **phrasing**, or when to pause. Paying attention to phrasing can also make the poem's meaning clearer.

Page 159

Teeth like jackhammers,
I chew through concrete for fun,
bring the outdoors in!

The commas in this poem signal places to pause when reading.

The exclamation point signals a place to show expression and excitement.

Your Turn Turn back to page 158. Take turns reading "Chimpanzee" aloud with a partner. Pay attention to the punctuation. Visualize what is happening in the poem. How does the poet want the reader to feel? Express your feelings in the way you read the poem.

Afterward, think about how you did. Complete these sentences.

I remembered to _____

_____

Next time I will _____

_____

WRITING

Expert Model

Literature Anthology:
Pages 132–137

Features of a Lyric Poem

A lyric poem is usually a short rhythmic poem that expresses a feeling instead of telling a story. A lyric poem

- expresses the thoughts or feelings of the poet

- often has end rhymes and a consistent meter

- is written in stanzas

Word Wise

On page 133, poet X.J. Kennedy uses words such as *darkens, forage, juicy, meaty,* and *scary* to describe the bats, their food, and the animals' actions. These words help paint a picture of the bats as predators.

Analyze an Expert Model Studying lyric poetry will help you learn how to write a lyric poem. **Reread** "Bat" on page 133 in the **Literature Anthology**. Write your answers below.

Reread the last stanza. How does the poet feel about bats? _____

_____

_____

What do the meter and rhyme contribute to the tone or mood of

the poem? _____

_____

_____

_____

Plan: Choose Your Topic

Brainstorm With a partner or a small group, brainstorm a list of animals, insects, or plants that you feel strongly about. Add one or two descriptive details about each item on the list. Use these discussion starters to help you brainstorm.

My favorite animal is _____

This plant has _____

The insect is interesting because _____

Writing Prompt Write a lyric poem about an animal, an insect, or a plant that you feel strongly about.

I will write about _____

Purpose and Audience An **author's purpose** is his or her main reason for writing. Look at the three purposes for writing below. Underline your purpose for writing a lyric poem.

   to inform, or teach   to persuade, or convince   to entertain

Think about the **audience** for your poem. Who will read it?

My audience will be _____.

Plan In your writer's notebook, use a word web to plan your writing. Put the topic in the center circle. Fill in the circles with your thoughts and feelings.

> ### Quick Tip
>
> As you get ready to write, close your eyes and pretend that you are the animal, insect, or plant that you chose. Now use your senses: how do things look, sound, feel, taste, or smell? Make a list of these sensory details.

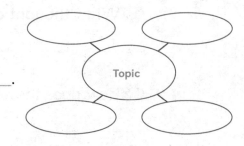

Plan: Stanza

Organize Your Poem When you write a story, you put your sentences into paragraphs connected by events. In a poem, you use stanzas: two or more lines that form a unit. Poets often use stanzas to start a new thought. Read the lyric poem below.

The Nautilus
The strangest creature in the sea?
Some say the eight-legged octopus.
The oddest always seemed to me
To be the baffling nautilus.

He peeks out from his spiral shell
While sailing on a backward trip.
He doesn't seem to know too well
How best to steer his puzzling ship.

1 What thought does the poet express in the first stanza? _____

_____

2 How does the second stanza support the idea in the first stanza? _____

_____

Organization In your writer's notebook, begin to plan your stanzas. Choose details from your word web and organize them into groups. These groups will be the base for each of your stanzas.

Draft

Rhyme Lyric poets use rhyme to make their language sound more musical and to give their poems rhythm. In this example from "Eagle," the poet uses rhyming words such as *crawls, walls,* and *falls* to make the language of his poem sing.

> The wrinkled sea beneath him crawls;
> He watches from his mountain walls,
> And like a thunderbolt he falls.

Now use the above stanza as a model to write about the topic you chose for your poem. Remember to use rhyming words so that your poem sings!

_____

_____

_____

_____

_____

_____

_____

Write a Draft Use your word web, groups of details, and the stanza you wrote above to help you draft your poem. Use the same arrangement of syllables in each line to help give your poem a consistent meter.

Revise

Assonance Lyric poets use words in creative and musical ways. Assonance is a tool writers use to make language appeal to your sense of hearing. Assonance is the use of the same vowel sound in a line or verse. Say the following sentence aloud to hear what assonance sounds like.

I like to ride my bike.

What vowel sound is repeated five times in the sentence above?

_____

Reread the lines from the poem "Deer" below. Then underline the words that have the long *e* sound in them.

> The headlights turn their dark eyes green.
> We see them sitting under trees
> At night, in my yard, like a photo of my family.

How does the author's use of assonance make the poem more interesting

to the reader? _____

_____

 Revision Revise your draft, and add some assonance to make the language in your poem sound more musical. Assonance can also slow down or speed up the pace of your words.

Word Wise

There is a difference between rhyming words and assonance. Assonance does not have to rhyme. Remember, use rhyme with care and only when it adds meaning to your poem. Sometimes less is more!

Peer Conferences

Review a Draft Listen carefully as a partner reads aloud his or her work. Take notes about what you liked and what was difficult to follow. Begin by telling what you liked about the draft. Ask questions that will help the writer think more about the writing. Make suggestions you think will make the writing stronger. Use these sentence starters.

I enjoyed the way you described your thoughts because . . .

I think you could end this stanza here because . . .

I don't see examples of assonance. You could add some . . .

Partner Feedback After your partner gives you feedback on your draft, write one of the suggestions that you will use in your revision. Refer to the rubric on page 183 as you give feedback.

Based on my partner's feedback, I will _____

_____

After you finish giving each other feedback, reflect on the peer conference. What was helpful? What might you do differently next time?

Revision As you revise your draft, use the Revising Checklist to help you figure out what text you may need to move, elaborate on, or delete. Remember to use the rubric on page 183 to help with your revision.

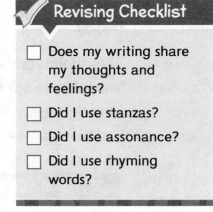

Revising Checklist

☐ Does my writing share my thoughts and feelings?

☐ Did I use stanzas?

☐ Did I use assonance?

☐ Did I use rhyming words?

Edit and Proofread

When you edit and proofread your writing, you look for and correct mistakes in spelling, punctuation, capitalization, and grammar. Reading through a revised draft multiple times can help you make sure you're catching any errors. Use the checklist below to edit your sentences.

Grammar Connections

When you proofread your poem, check for common spelling mistakes. For example, *alright* should be *all right* and *alot* should be *a lot*.

✔ Editing Checklist

- ☐ Do your pronouns agree with the nouns they refer to?
- ☐ Is there a space between the stanzas?
- ☐ Is there subject and verb agreement?
- ☐ Are possessive nouns and contractions used correctly?
- ☐ Are all words spelled correctly?

List two mistakes you found as you proofread your poem.

1 _____

_____

2 _____

_____

Publish, Present, and Evaluate

Publishing As you write your final draft, be sure to write legibly in cursive. Check that you are holding your pencil or pen correctly between your finger and thumb. This will help you **publish** a neat final copy.

Presentation When you are ready to **present** your work, rehearse your presentation. Use the Presenting Checklist to help you.

Evaluate After you publish your writing, use the rubric below to **evaluate** your writing.

What did you do successfully? _____

_____

_____

What needs more work? _____

_____

_____

✓ Presenting Checklist

- ☐ Stand up straight.
- ☐ Look at the audience.
- ☐ Speak slowly and clearly.
- ☐ Speak loud enough for everyone to hear you.
- ☐ Make sure your tone matches the emotions you are presenting in your poem.

4	3	2	1
• expresses feelings and ideas in an original way • is complete and organized into lines and stanzas • few or no errors in spelling and punctuation	• expresses feelings and ideas • is mostly complete and organized into lines and stanzas • some errors in spelling and punctuation	• expresses some feelings or an idea • has attempted to put some lines into stanzas • a number of errors in spelling and punctuation	• writing includes a feeling or an idea • lines do not appear to be organized • many errors in spelling and punctuation

Spiral Review

You have learned new skills and strategies in Unit 2 that will help you read more critically. Now it is time to practice what you have learned.

- **Antonyms**
- **Elements of a Play**
- **Hyperbole**
- **Make Inferences**
- **Main Idea and Details**
- **Prefixes**
- **Photographs and Captions**
- **Theme**

Connect to Content

- **Research an Endangered Habitat**
- **Write a Comic Strip**
- **Read Digitally**

Read the selection and choose the best answer to each question.

Nine-Banded Armadillos

1   The armadillo is the official state small mammal of Texas. In Spanish, *armadillo* means "little armored one." The only living mammal that has this unique protection, they are the relative of anteaters and sloths. Despite its name, the nine-banded armadillo can have between seven and eleven bands. They sleep all day and like to be by themselves.

Life Cycle

2   A mother armadillo carries her babies for roughly four months. Then she gives birth in a burrow. Nine-banded armadillos usually birth four identical pups. By the time they are a year old, the pups are fully grown. An average armadillo is about 2.5 feet long and weighs about 12 pounds. In the wild, they live between 7 and 20 years.

Habitat

3   Armadillos do not have a lot of body fat. Therefore, they like warm climates, including rain forests, grasslands, and semi-deserts. Of the twenty species of armadillo, all but one live in Latin America. The nine-banded variety is the only one found in the United States. They can be found in Texas and as far north as Illinois.

Diet

4 Armadillos are omnivores, which means their diet includes meat and vegetables. They have poor eyesight, so they rely on their keen sense of smell. With their pointy snouts, armadillos can find almost 500 different foods! Much of their diet consists of insects, though. Armadillos eat some fruit, seeds, and fungi. Sometimes, they scavenge for dead animals. Most forage in the early morning and evening, when enemies are sleeping.

Defense and Armor

5 Imagine a rabbit with armor, and you have the Texas state small mammal. The armadillo's bony shields are made of overlapping plates. Armadillos' one weakness: a soft belly. Their enemies include dogs, alligators, coyotes, and humans. When scared, they sometimes hide, showing only their shells. Nine-banded armadillos jump up about three to four feet into the air when startled!

Habits

6 These animals could be called <u>antisocial</u> because they like to be alone. In fact, armadillos spend most of their time sleeping. They do get together to mate and to keep warm. Despite their armor, they aren't afraid of the water. By inflating their stomachs, armadillos can float. Some have been known to hold their breath for six minutes or more.

The bands of armor on an armadillo are jointed, allowing it to bend.

Armadillo Day, February 2

What do Texans do on Groundhog Day in a state without groundhogs? Have Armadillo Day, of course! Started in 2012, the Lone Star Weatherological Society hosts the gathering near Austin. Every year, people gather for the famed forecast. At 12:30 p.m. people bring Bee Cave Bob out of his burrow. If he stays, spring is near. If he goes back, there's going to be more winter.

Deborah Cannon/Austin American-Statesman/AP Images

Early spring? Six weeks more of winter? Only Bee Cave Bob, the armadillo, knows!

1. Which sentence expresses the main idea of paragraph 4?

   A Poor eyesight makes it hard for an armadillo to see its food.

   B Armadillos eat only insects.

   C Morning and evening are the best times for armadillos to find food.

   D Armadillos are omnivores.

2. The prefix *anti-* means "against" or "opposite of."

   This information helps the reader know that the word <u>antisocial</u> in paragraph 6 means —

   F wanting to be around others.

   G not wanting to be around others.

   H leaving others behind.

   J following others where they go.

3. The photograph and caption about Bee Cave Bob helps readers understand that —

   A armadillos are a part of Texas culture today.

   B armadillos like winter.

   C the man found an armadillo near Bee Cave, Texas.

   D Bee Cave is a home for many armadillo populations.

> **Quick Tip**
>
> Reread the caption under the photograph on page 185. Which answer does the caption best support?

4. Readers can infer that the author thinks armadillos are —

   F going to replace the sloth and anteater populations.

   G a threat to humans in the southern United States.

   H interesting animals.

   J lazy animals because they sleep most of the day.

Read the selection and choose the best answer to each question.

PAUL MEETS BABE, THE BLUE OX

CHARACTERS
Narrator
Paul Bunyan
Babe

1   (Setting: Bangor, Maine; deep in the woods in the dead of winter.)

2   (PAUL BUNYAN, dressed in a flannel shirt, walks carrying an ax over his shoulder.)

3   NARRATOR: It was the dead of winter in the Blue Snow. Paul Bunyan, a giant of a man, and lumberjack supreme, had just finished his day of timbering. He was mighty hungry after tossing boulders around and pulling up trees to make a new trail through the forest. Of course, he had some fun juggling the boulders, too! Now he was headed back to the lodge.

4   PAUL: (to himself, while he walks) I wonder what's for supper! Right about now I could eat fifty pots of Tom's beef stew and twenty loaves of bread!

3   (PAUL sets down the ax and pulls out a small lunch sack from his pants pocket. Shakes it out to see if there is anything left.) This teeny tiny lunch definitely wasn't enough for my enormous appetite!

6   NARRATOR: In the distance, Paul hears a sound. Paul's hearing was so good, he could hear a pin drop in China.

7   (An animal snorts, angrily.)

8   PAUL: (looks up, startled) Hello? Is someone there?

9   NARRATOR: Concerned that someone was hurt, Paul went to investigate.

10   (PAUL starts walking toward the bleating to discover BABE, a small ox, who jumps up and down in the snow, trying to see over the drift.)

11   PAUL: Now, what have we here? Aren't you a spunky critter! What is a little ox doing out in these parts? You're thinner than a toothpick! (Paul pets his head, carefully and tenderly.) And you're all covered in blue from the snow. Got your tail in a twist because you're too short to see over the towering drift?

12   (BABE continues to snort angrily.)

13   PAUL: You know, this wind is a mite chilly. It's so frigid in these parts, I've seen polar bears wear jackets! Let's go back to the lodge and get toasty. We'll put you in front of the fire. If we wait too long, you might stay as blue as this snow!

14   NARRATOR: And Paul, that gentle giant, carried the small blue-stained ox all the way back to the lodge. But even after the little ox was warmed and fed, he remained blue! So Paul named his new friend Babe, the Blue Ox.

Which of the following is the purpose of stage directions?

A   explain what characters do on stage

B   list the names of the characters

C   tell what the characters say

D   tell how much dialogue there will be

② Which of the following is an antonym for the word <u>towering</u> in paragraph 11?

F   spunky

G   short

H   covered

J   thin

③ The theme of this scene in the play is that —

A   the Blue Snow is a dangerous and cold place.

B   even a giant lumberjack can be a caring and gentle person.

C   lumberjacks usually have an ox for a friend.

D   small oxen sometimes get lost in the snow.

④ An example of hyperbole in paragraph 13 is —

F   Let's go back to the lodge.

G   You know, this wind is a mite chilly.

H   We'll put you in front of the fire.

J   It's so frigid in these parts, I've seen polar bears wear jackets!

Readers to Writers

Plays are written to be performed, but they include more than dialogue. A play's structure helps you learn more about the characters, where they are, and what they are doing. The descriptions in the cast list at the beginning of a play can help you visualize the characters. Character names tell which character is speaking. The text is often divided into acts and scenes; they tell when and where the action takes place and often signal the beginning or end of a situation.

Quick Tip

The theme is the message or lesson. To figure out the theme, look at what the character says and does.

EXTEND YOUR LEARNING

PREFIXES AND SUFFIXES

COLLABORATE

A **prefix** is added to the beginning of a word and changes the meaning of the word. A **suffix** is added to the end of a word and changes the word's meaning, too. A suffix may also change the spelling of the base word or a word's part of speech. Here are some common prefixes and suffixes.

Prefixes

sub- means "under" or "below"
    plot, subplot

mis- means "wrongly" or "not"
    judge, misjudge

Suffixes

-ity/-ty means "state or quality of"
    humid, humidity

-ment means "action or process"
    agree, agreement

- Add a prefix or a suffix to the base words below. Write the new word and its definition.

- Use a print or an online dictionary to check your words.

Base Word	New Word	Definition
achieve		
behave		
enjoy		
loyal		
marine		
spell		
pure		
way		

FIGURATIVE LANGUAGE

COLLABORATE

Figurative language is a word or phrase that writers use to create images in the reader's mind. There are several kinds of figurative language.

- **Similes** compare two unlike things, using *like* or *as*.
  Example: *Her smile was as bright as the sun.*
  Meaning: Her smile was warm and friendly.

- **Metaphors** compare two unlike things, without using *like* or *as*.
  Example: *Her smile was the sun.*
  Meaning: Her smile was very bright and warm.

- **Personification** gives animals, ideas, or objects human qualities.
  Example: *The sun smiled down on the land.*
  Meaning: The sun was shining on the land.

With a partner, identify the figurative language in each sentence below. Write the meaning of the figurative language. Then write your own sentence, using figurative language.

Three skunks were chattering in the yard.

Figure of speech: _____

Meaning: _____

Your Sentence: _____

The daffodil was as yellow as a lemon.

Figure of speech: _____

Meaning: _____

Your Sentence: _____

Bill McMullen/Moment/Getty Images

MAKE A PODCAST

A podcast is a digital audio file that can be shared with others. Many podcasts are educational, teaching the listeners about a topic that interests them.

- Research an endangered animal habitat in your state. Use print and online materials for your research.

- Make a podcast explaining why the habitat is endangered and what people can do to help protect it.

Write what you learned below.

I chose this endangered habitat because _____

_____

One way to help this endangered habitat is _____

_____

Quick Tip

A digital environment allows you to use different methods to tell more about the animals that interest you. You can use a mixture of photographs, illustrations, audio, and explanatory text to turn a research project into a multimodal presentation. If your class has a blog or website, you might post your comic strip and podcast recording to the site.

WRITE A COMIC STRIP

A comic strip is a set of illustrations or drawings that are placed in a certain order to tell a story. They can be found in books and newspapers.

- Research facts about two animals that interest you.

- Draw a comic strip about the animals. Using dialogue balloons, write dialogue for the animals in your comic strip.

My favorite part about writing a comic strip is _____

_____

SHARKS UNDER ATTACK

COLLABORATE

SCIENCE

Log on to **my.mheducation.com** and reread the online *Time For Kids* article "Sharks Under Attack." Pay attention to the information found in the interactive elements. Answer the questions below.

Sharks Under Attack
Shark populations around the world are shrinking. Steps are being taken to save the fish before it's too late.

Time for Kids: Sharks Under Attack

- Why is it difficult for the shark population to come back from overfishing? Use information from the article and the linked Global Shark Conservation web page.

  _____

  _____

- What important role do sharks play in the ecosystem?

  _____

  _____

- Look at the diagram of the shark's body. How do the fins on a shark help it to survive?

  _____

  _____

- What other adaptations do sharks have that help them survive?

  _____

  _____

tswinner/iStock/Getty Images

TRACK YOUR PROGRESS

WHAT DID YOU LEARN?

Use the rubric to evaluate yourself on the skills that you learned in this unit. Write your scores below.

4	3	2	1
I can successfully identify all examples of this skill.	I can identify most examples of this skill.	I can identify a few examples of this skill.	I need to work on this skill more.

☐ Main Idea and Details   ☐ Theme   ☐ Point of View

☐ Prefixes   ☐ Antonyms   ☐ Similes and Metaphors

Something that I need to work more on is _____ because

_____

_____

_____

Text to Self Think back over the texts that you have read in this unit. Choose one text and write a short paragraph explaining a personal connection that you have made to the text.

I made a personal connection to _____ because _____

_____

_____

SCIENCE

Present Your Work

COLLABORATE

Discuss how you will present your digital poster about the animal you researched. As you present, point out the details in the poster. Tell the sources for your facts by using your bibliography. Use the Presenting Checklist as you practice your presentation. Discuss the sentence starters below and write your answers.

An unusual fact that I learned about my animal is _____

_____

_____

_____

I would like to know more about _____

_____

_____

_____

Eric Gevaert/Getty Images

Quick Tip

If you include video, you can insert a hyperlink onto your digital poster. Make sure the hyperlink is still live before you give your presentation.

✓ Presenting Checklist

☐ Rehearse your presentation in front of a friend. Ask for feedback.

☐ Time the presentation to make sure it is just the right length.

☐ Emphasize important information so the audience can follow.

☐ Make eye contact with the people in the audience.

☐ Remember to share your bibliography.